The Rainbows Inside of Me

A Latin Woman's Story
of
Life, Love and Hope

T.L. León

Published by P.F. & Associates

ISBN 13: 978-0-9769772-3-0

Manufactured in the United States of America

Cover Photography by Christopher Bossio/Bossio Photography

Cover Design and Interior Layout by Jessica Tilles/TWA Solutions

Author Photography by Maegan C. Paniewski

Printed in the United States of America

This book is dedicated to all the Hispanic/Latin women who have never been heard.

You are Beautiful.

You are Strong.

You are Deserving!

The Rainbows Inside of Me

A Latin Woman's Story
of
Life, Love and Hope

Preface

Have you felt like you had it altogether? That you were at a good place in your life? That whatever happened in your past, you had dealt with it and you see someone else going through something you've gone through and said, "Oh yeah, been there, done that, bought a t-shirt and the rest of the store?"

You see, I have always been told that I was a strong, loud, ambitious Puerto Rican—well, Nuyorican woman. That I was REAL and that was what some liked about me. I didn't take any stuff, per se. But at the same time, I would give you the shirt off my back and be there to pick up the pieces when you fell apart.

I was always the person who looked out for everybody else and never let you know what was going on inside me. Everyone knew when I was quiet or didn't say much that I needed my space. They would say, "Leave her alone," or "She'll figure it out and she'll let you know if and when she needs something." Well, this is how my story begins...

At the age of fifteen, and being the good catholic girl I was raised to be, I got involved in the youth program at my church. I loved it and went on my first Encuentro Con Cristo. I loved it so much, I worked more and more with the Encuentro's until I became the youngest Assistant Director the Encuentro's had ever had. I was sixteen. An honor I felt privileged to have and I would wear my "Cuito" religiously (no pun intended), the Encuentro's nickname for Jesus. I even wore it outside my Catholic school uniform, often being teased by kids in school. I didn't care; I loved my Heavenly Father and wanted everyone to know it.

The summer of the end of my junior year in high school, I was invited to attend a retreat representing various churches in upstate New York. I was so excited. I went willingly, of course, with other members from my diocese that I knew. During this week, I was asked to perform in a skit that displayed the temptations of life. I played a prostitute in this skit. Apparently, I became the gossip of the boys retreat that it got back to my church. These young men had left early to participate in their parish retreat leaving them plenty of time to talk shit about me.

After the retreat, I left for a job at a summer camp and didn>t know anything about this until I received a letter from the nun at my church, telling me how disappointed she was, what a sin I had committed, I was supposed to be an example for other teens and how could I do such a thing. I was devastated and cried for hours, feeling that now the church was against me. I never felt the same about her, church, the members of the youth group. It left me feeling ashamed and embarrassed. I didn't want to return to church and started to move away from the church. In not feeling the support of the church, I felt abandoned, betrayed and out casted.

At the age of seventeen, I left home for college and fell in love with a man that I had met. I became pregnant my freshman year in college. Scared and confused, I came home during spring break and broke the news to my parents that I was pregnant. My parents were devastated. They cursed me and belittled me. They forced me to have an abortion and feeling guilty about hurting my parents, I did as they wished me to do. Again, ashamed, embarrassed and abandoned.

A few months later, I decided to leave home to be with the man I loved. My family cursed me and told me if I walked out that door I would be dead to them and not to talk, write or communicate with anyone they knew. I was dead to them! The hate that spewed from their lips that day left me lost, confused and yet determined to find my way. I feel I had nothing to lose. I had already lost everything else. This just felt right and fulfilled that emptiness I had been having.

We moved in together. Well, it wasn›t exactly the happy ending you would have expected. He was eleven years my senior, had been married before and had a child. He had known things I hadn›t even experienced yet. But I loved him and was determined to make it work. He was a good man, a good provider, and a good father. So I thought.

Things at the beginning were rough. We struggled at first, trying to get to know each other, and I was living without a support system, which made it harder for me. I missed my family, but knew I could never go home. I had no one to talk to, write to, cry with or even laugh with. My heart was heavy.

Things started to get really difficult and one day I decided I needed to get away. I joined the military — like my father — and felt that this was the answer. After much arguing and fighting with the man I loved and his family, I left for the Army. Letters went back and forth between him and me while I was away in Boot Camp. Some good, some bad, but when boot camp ended, I was assigned to a base back home and I went back to him and a few months later I became pregnant. What was supposed to have been a joyous time wasn›t. The abuse I received from this man, the man I was in love with and whom I thought was in love with me, was shocking. He hit me a few times, yelled at me and just made me feel like the most insignificant person on the planet. Okay, it wasn›t always that bad, but it happened more than it should have. We were financially strapped; baby on the way and my father-in-law was dying. He was under a lot of stress

I was feeling lost and no one to turn to not even God. God, what did I do so badly for You to leave me?

A beautiful baby boy was born to us one summer day in July, and finally he became the man I always thought he would be.

Two years later, I became pregnant again, and the stress level intensified two-fold. He didn›t want the baby. In so many words, he wanted to abort the baby. "How could I put them through this again?" he had told me. No money, place too small, his oldest son from his first marriage was living with us it just wasn't the right time. "Get rid of it," he said. In my heart of hearts, I had already begun to love this child and refused to give it up. I was hoping for a little girl this time. In the month of September, another beautiful baby boy was born.

When our first child was born to us, I was able to reconnect with my family and slowly, but surely, my parents accepted the situation and accepted me and my husband and our beautiful baby boys back into their lives, and finally I felt whole. I never told my family the abuse I had incurred with this man up to that point, but I was still determined to make our life work.

Over the next several years, I suffered from depression, anxiety and couldn›t even get out of bed. At one point, I was placed on suicide watch. I even had to go out on short-term disability from my job. I would often ask, "Where is God?" I believed in Him so much at one time. What did I do to lose Him? Where can I find Him?

As time went by, it became more and more obvious my marriage wasn›t going to work. After a big fight, he left for good. Separation proceedings began and I got stronger and stronger every day, but my struggles became deeper and much more difficult.

My husband challenged every move I made. He didn›t pay child support, electricity would be disconnected leaving me to borrow power from the electricity outside my apartment and then not pay the rent to be able to feed my children — almost being evicted twice.

Even, after the divorce was final, it still didn›t stop . I was charged with child abuse, our children›s visitation changed and my ex refused to accept that our oldest son suffered ADHD and denied him his medication.

"God where are You?" I couldn't find Him. I felt I had abandoned Him, so He punished me by leaving me.

One day, as I was taking a shortcut home, I came upon a Catholic church. My heart was heavy and I had to go in. Inside, I found the peace I had been longing for, and I started going back to church that Sunday, hoping to find God again.

The struggles of raising my children on my own were difficult—from almost being homeless, to rape, to incarceration, the issues with my ex-husband, job loss, depression and anxiety.

"GOD, GIVE ME THE STRENGTH TO CONROL THE THINGS I CAN, UNDERSTAND THE THINGS I CANT AND BELIEVE THAT THIS SITUATION IS TEMPORARY." Right????????

Chapter 1

"Walk with the wise and become wise,
for a companion of fools suffers harm.

—*Proverbs 13:20 (NIV)*

Part 1

How did I get here, again? I don't believe this! Didn't I just go through this last year, my heart torn out and stomped on like a butcher tenderizing meat? I mean, really. Okay, calm down. Relax. I'm not the same person I was last year. I have found peace. I am strong. I am calm. I will…. Breathe, breathe, breathe.

Okay, did he just say he still had feelings for her? Did he say he didn't understand what he was feeling, that he needed to figure it out? That he didn't want to play games with me, that he felt that I didn't deserve it, etc., etc., etc.?

His nickname was Tee. But I didn't meet him that way. Funny thing was I liked his online name, but that wasn't even his real name. Since he didn't like his God-given name by his parents, he chose to rename himself to what he wanted to be known as. But I thought his name was very regal, so I always called him by his first name that his parents gave him.

He is a handsome man, whom I initially wasn't really interested in. In fact, I wasn't really interested in meeting anyone. I was content with my life at that point. I had a terrible breakup the year before and really wasn't looking to meet anyone. He was pretty insistent, so I met him for lunch, which turned into dinner and then late night drinks as we watched the basketball playoffs together. He liked basketball and so did I and several of our dates revolved around the games. I think I really started to like him the first night he kissed my neck. I melted underneath him. I thought he was going to have to grab me just to hold me up. He was a romantic. Candles, music, massage; very much into pleasing me. Our first night together, I was suffering from a severe sunburn, but he knew what to do without my having to say anything. He was good like that.

He always made love to me. He always got the mood just right and there were times I felt like his eyes were piercing through my soul the way he would look at me when we made love. He was gentle yet strong. There were times he would whisper in my ear and my body would just melt. He knew what he did to me, that was for sure.

As time went on, we learned we had a lot more in common, things I didn't expect at all. Like the music he played in his car. I would just start singing and he was amazed at how many of the songs I knew. He even said to me one time that he didn't think anyone knew that version of a particular song playing. We had so much in common it was like he was the male version of me. And back then, I was afraid I wouldn't be able to fall in love with him.

I know it had only been three months, but damn, I asked myself what happened even though he told me it wasn't me. It had nothing to do with me. That I was great and he did care for me. That I was everything he wanted, but he was still having feelings for this other woman, whom, by the way, treated him like shit. He didn't think it was fair to me to "Not be into me, like I was into him." But when I did ask him how he felt about me, he hesitated.

"Wow," I said.

Then, of course, he said, "I care about you," and paused, which had nothing to do with it. He just couldn't say he loved me. Duh...

"It had only been three months," I said, and I didn't expect him to say that he loved me, but at least not hesitate in saying he cared about me. We talked for two hours about the situation, and I asked, "But, why? Why would you want to go back to that? I don't get it."

It took me three months to finally give in to him, and all I remember are my friends telling me: "Let go, girl!" and "He seems like a great guy!" and "Allow yourself to truly accept what this man is giving you because you, of all people, deserve to be happy." Imagine that. I held out so long because there were things about him that didn't add up or I just couldn't put my finger on it. So while we were enjoying each other, I just kept waiting for that bomb to drop, AND HELLO, BOY DID IT.

⊸┝═◉

"Oh, my God, it feels like I haven't seen you in forever. Give me a big hug." He had a surprise for me. I was so delighted he was in a good mood. He didn't seem like he was too happy when I spoke to him last night after the retreat. In fact, he was downright cold via text. I left it alone. And when I got home, I spoke to my son and went to bed, as those retreats wear me out.

When he called me earlier that day, saying he wanted to take me out and he had a surprise, I was thrilled. He took me to a Cuban/Puerto Rican restaurant that he figured I would love, and I really did. The food was great. We talked and he told me he had a horrible weekend, and was alone at the shop and didn't have any coverage so he was doing everything and I know that must have been crazy especially on the weekends. Well, that explained his mood the day before, I thought. He worked every other weekend and was really upset that no one paid attention to how the schedule was done. But being the manager, he was going to have to start reviewing all schedules again to be sure they were done right, etc.

In any case, after we left the restaurant, he came to my house. We started to "make love" — he never called it anything else. He hated calling it anything else. And he grabbed both my feet and starting kissing them so ever lightly. Now mind you, I was just coming off a retreat where we talked about Mary washing Jesus' feet and the meaning behind it. I thought I had died and gone to heaven. No, this man had not just grabbed my feet, massaged them and then kissed them. All I could do was cry and cry and cry. He held me in his arms.

"What's wrong?" he asked.

"Nothing," I said.

It was so beautiful to me. No one had ever done that to me. I gave myself to him freely that night. I felt then it was okay to give him my soul and begin falling in love with him.

The next week, I planned a surprise "drive-by" at his job with dinner. I decorated a box with Zebra wrap, bought his favorite chicken dinner at a local fast-food restaurant and drove forty-five minutes to his job. I was so excited, but scared to death at the same time. You know guys don't like girls showing up at their job unannounced, but whatever. He was truly surprised and was grateful. I waited about a half an hour until he got out of work and we went to his house. He decided to plan our trip to New York for my birthday. I was so excited. We reserved a hotel, flights and even the rental car. Awesome and we made incredible love. Wow, I thought, maybe I should bring him dinner more often. Although, I often would cook at his house as we got ready to watch our favorite TV series.

That Friday night, we got hit by a Tropical Storm. The state wasn't the only thing that got hit by the Tropical Storm that weekend. My own turbulent storm hit me that Sunday night.

Part 2

"Well, I guess I'm not going to New York with you?"

"I don't know, you tell me? Are you going back to her?"

Tee said, "I realized that I can't go back to that situation. It's unhealthy for me and nothing really has changed. But I can't keep the same type of relationship with you."

"Okay, what the hell does that mean, 'The same type of relationship'?"

Was he kidding me? A week had gone by and that was the best he could do. I didn't bother him; I left him to do what he asked me to do. And the best he could do was this. It took everything in me to not lose my mind.

"Are you in love with this woman?" I asked him.

"Yes, I still am."

WOW.

The BOMB had officially dropped. After I shared so much with him about my previous relationship and told him how much I was in love with, what's his name... oh yea, Miguel and how I was broken into a million pieces, and he couldn't tell me he was in love with his last girlfriend. Oh, and let's not forget they were only apart when we first met five months ago and now at this point eight months.

I stayed cool, calm and collected, and said to him that it would have been nice if he had told me that earlier and maybe the relationship would have been different and I would not have gotten involved as deeply. I wasn't in love with him yet, but I had just released myself to do so. I suggested he take more time out for himself and figure things out before he got involved with anyone again, as that was the only way I was able to move on. Life was complicated enough without bringing other people's drama into yours.

Now, everything made sense — the little funny issues (my own observations), the missing acts, the sometimes solemnness of his day. I don't know, maybe I was looking for excuses for trying to understand all this craziness. What made it worse was that I understood what he was going through. At least he was honest with me and told me before anything happened and didn't have me floating in the wind somewhere. I felt bad for him and told him if he ever needed someone to talk to that I would be there and try to support him. I really meant it, too.

It felt so right. How could this happen to me again? For sure, I knew it wasn't me. I did everything right this time or at least I thought I did. I didn't pressure him to define the relationship, we enjoyed each other tremendously. We never fought. We shared everything, and he even washed my clothes for me. No man has ever done that for me. He knew how to make me feel like a goddess, a princess, and a queen.

After the first week we met, he left on a cruise with his cousin for a weekend and he brought me back two bracelets and a blue fish with big red lips. Not sure what he was trying to say with the red lips, but it was the thought that counted and I was thrilled. It was the little things that made me happy. Another time, after about a month of dating, he sent me an eCard that read: *If beliefs are strong enough, and dreams are set free... Then thoughts will find their way, and wishes will come true. ALWAYS LIVE BETTER THAN YESTERDAY!*

I remember asking him why he had done so much for me and his answer was "You Deserve It!" Damn right I did. But I didn't deserve being left like this. Not for another woman who had treated him like crap and left him on the side of the curb, not fighting for her man. I would have fought for him. He was a good guy. He really was, but I couldn't change a heart that was hell-bent on trying to figure out what happened with the last relationship. Why do we need to find closure when there may not be a logical explanation for why people do what they do? I never got closure on my last relationship, but I left it up to the universe to resolve that issue because there are just some things you can't change, no matter how much you try and some things you just miss the boat on and that boat isn't coming back to that port ever again.

I can't say I was devastated totally, but I was hurt, shocked and in disbelief. "Always live better than yesterday....." as I posted the e-card on my cork board so

I would see it every day and remind me of him... yeah, right. Look who ISN'T living better than yesterday.

So I asked myself: What is the lesson learned here? What did I experience and what was the reason for this relationship?

Chapter 2

✺

"Don't just pretend to love others. Really love them. Hate what is wrong. Hold tightly to what is good."

—*Romans 12:9 (NLT)*

Part 1

*W*hat a beautiful little girl, and your son is adorable. Of course, I'll keep them. I'll treat them like my own."

They were a large family. Three girls and four boys. All I could think of is what a lot of kids to play with. I was in nursery school and would go to Dona Garcia's house after school. My little brother stayed with her all day as he was way too young to go to school yet. All the other kids went off to school, too, which I didn't like very much because I would be ready to play and they wouldn't be home yet, or had homework to do.

Their oldest son stayed home, but he was very different. He had a room up in the attic and was, to me, quite unsocial. I barely saw him, at least from what I remembered. But then again I was about four years old at the time.

For the most part, things were pretty normal. I brought my toys over to play so when my brother would be napping, or when nursery school ended, I would have something to do.

Nursery school was interesting because it seemed like I was the only Latina in the classroom. Being four years old, I didn't know that people could be prejudice and didn't even know what the hell that meant, so I remember not really caring for the teacher too much and that experience has stayed with me.

I remember we were going to lunch, and we would each go into the bathrooms and wash our hands before eating. I have a birth mark on my index finger. A little brown dot. That teacher made me scrub my hands until I couldn't wash them anymore, and she yelled at me saying I didn't wash my hands good enough and that is why that dirty spot stayed there. I remember crying to Mami when she came to pick me up at school about the spot on my hand and asked her why I was so different. After wiping my eyes and explaining that I wasn't different and the birth mark on my finger was a gift that showed how special I was, I began to feel better. Being the true Latina mom that she was, she ran right into that classroom after she saw that I was better and WWIII broke out. Mami cussed that teacher out in a very professional way and I never had to worry about going back to that school after that. In fact, I never did go back.

Since I wasn't going to nursery school anymore, I spent all day at Dona's house. One day, while taking a nap, her oldest son snuck into the room He picked me up and laid me on top of him. I didn't know what to do. I was half asleep and wasn't sure what was going on so I didn't make a move. I could feel his chest rise and fall. It was a very uncomfortable feeling and I was too afraid to open my eyes as I didn't know what his reaction would have been. After a while, he would then lay me back on the bed and I would fall back asleep. That wasn't the first nor the last time he did that, and out of fear and maybe no one to believe me,

The oddness of the activities among the kids in that house, didn't end there.

As time went by, when some of the other kids got home from school, they would play with me and my brother. Often times, Dona would be cooking or cleaning so the older kids would come in and help take care of me and my brother. There were times that I would see the brothers and sisters doing things with each other that seemed different from the regular games other kids played, but they were older so I didn't know any better. They called it "Playing Doctor." Touching here and there with each other and often times I would peak through the door to see what was going on. One day, I was invited into the room. I lay on the bed and they started touching me. I don't remember being scared or sad as I trusted them and they did it to each other, so I guessed it was okay. But deep inside, I knew it wasn't, even at four years old, but was too afraid to move or say anything. I never told anyone about it or him for that matter.

This came to an end when I started attending elementary school I was then being taken care by another family closer to home.

Part 2

A few years later, a family moved in the neighborhood two doors down from where I lived. I was about eight or nine at the time. My brother had become friends with the youngest boy of the family and he was over there all the time.

One day, this boys sister came over with him to get my brother and she invited me over to play with her. Now, this was particularly interesting, because she never asked me to come over before, and since I had always wanted to hang out with her, I naturally went.

What happened next, I did not expect.

A group of the boys gathered in an upper room of the house, playing who knows what. As my newfound friend started going up the stairs she told me to follow her. We went into the room to see what was happening and discovered the boys messing around on the bed looking out the small window over the bed.

I wanted to see what they were looking at, so I climbed on the bed to look out the window and that's when it happened.

The boys wrestled me down on the bed, the suppose it new friend I found closed the door and that's when the fondling occurred. I don't remember how many boys were in there as I just closed my eyes and made pretend it was a game.

What seemed like a lifetime, ended with a call from downstairs from their mother. As the boys scrabbled around I jumped off the bed, put what ever clothes that were hanging off of me back on and ran out the door horrified. I was home within minutes and locked myself up in my room never to talk of it again. I never went back to that house, nor did I ever talk to that girl again.

Chapter 3

"His name was Nabal and his wife's name was
Abigail. She was an intelligent and beautiful woman, but
her husband was surly and mean in his dealings."
—1 Samuel 25:3 (NIV)

I need help with Math. I'm failing and I need a tutor, can you help me?" I asked him.

"Sure I can."

Not sure if he said it because he wanted to be with me or really wanted to help me. At this point I didn't care. I needed help and anyway I could get it.

I met him originally through this other guy I had met on campus. He totally became a top notch looser. He worked in the bookstore and hooked me up with some books for class and we started dating, until I walked to his place from campus one night and a girl answered the door. I should have known then. Talk about naïve. I never guessed he was staying with a girl, let alone his "girlfriend."

It took him forever to get to the door. I then figured out things after she kept telling him to go to the door and she came with him. I was like....okay, well, I didn't know, he never told me and he is all yours. As I was leaving, all hell broke loose and I heard some serious screaming, yelling and things being thrown around.

I was a little hesitant to talk to Leonard (nickname Lynn) because he was friends with this other guy, but we were in the university's play together, so I saw him every day. He seemed okay and I remember all the girls being crazy about him. He was one of the only guys in the play that was straight.

There was something about him. He definitely could dance his ass off which had me watching him. I didn't have a talking part in the play as I was just a dancer, and because Lynn was good and caught on fast to the steps, he would often work with me separately so I could get the steps down. Of course, all the other girls were jealous.

I can't remember when we first hooked up, but he definitely knew how to treat me. He was very lavish and sophisticated. He was always buying the best of things and always went high class.

One weekend he took me away to the Omni Hotel. I was so excited and just couldn't believe he had done that. He bought me a beautiful red dress, and shoes to match. "We are going out on the town," he said and I was ready. We had breakfast called in the next morning and we had mimosas. I had never had one before then and the champagne was J. Roget. I'll never forget it because I always looked for it years after we were married. Trying to relive that moment.

I knew he was older, but by how much I didn't know. Every time I asked him he would just blow it off and say, "Don't worry about it." Since I worked in the Financial Aid office, I had access to everyone's files. Not that I would abuse it or anything, but I really needed to know his age. So, I checked his file, and found out why he didn't want to tell me—eleven years older than me. I would have never guessed. He didn't look that old. But it did explain why he was the way he was; much more mature than some of the idiots that had approached me. I loved the way he treated me and I allowed him to indulge me in every way.

I remember something happening where he had to cancel a date with me and I was ready to go and I got upset with him. Not too long after that, he finally told me that he had been in the military and had been married, but that now he was divorced and had a son. Wow, a lot to swallow at one time. But I accepted him and later that week I met his son.

As time went on, I began to realize that I would have an instant family if things were to continue going in the direction they were going in.

Things were getting pretty serious and we had already started talking about getting married and our future together.

His son was a great kid and I really liked him. He was eight years old and filled with tons of energy. I could tell the relationship Lynn had with his son was special, but unfortunately the relationship with his ex-wife was not good at all. I wondered what happened, but didn't ask.

We spent a lot of time together and being that I was only ten years older than his son, I understood him pretty well and he was very smart for his age. I felt that I had found a man who could fulfill all my girlish dreams that I had at the time. At this point, I was in love with Lynn and I fell in love with his son, too. I often dreamed what life would be like with him and how much in love we were. It became my centering thought. Thus, my hell began.

Chapter 4

"No, my brother!" she said to him. "Don't force me!
Such a thing should not be done in Israel!
Don't do this wicked thing."
— 2 Samuel 13:12

*M*is padres came into the city the night before to visit my abuela and my titi that just had a baby a month ago. She lived in the same building as my abuela and I loved babies, so I asked Mami and Papi if I could stay with Titi to take care of the baby. They all agreed.

I was sleeping on the couch in the living room and was suddenly awakened.

"What time is it?" I asked.

"Who are you?" he asked me

"Your brother's wife's niece," I told him.

He didn't seem too smart to me. I had never met him before. It had to be close to sunrise because I could see the sunlight starting to come through the curtains, but it was still sort of gray outside.

I had asked him who he was and he told me he was my uncle's brother. We talked for a few minutes and then he told me he was just coming home from work since he worked in a night club. Since I had been sleeping, I was coming in and out of the conversation and missed some of what he was saying. He all of sudden made this announcement of "So, I guess you're family. That means you owe me a kiss."

He approached me and, as I was lifting myself up to a sitting position, lay on top of me and started thrusting his tongue in and out of my mouth. I began to panic as he held me down and wouldn't stop. I finally got enough strength to push him off me. He was on top of me on the edge of the couch and I jumped up and ran into Titi's room.

Both she and her husband jumped up as I practically startled them to death because I was crying hysterically. I tried to tell them what had happened between my tears, and Tio told me to stay in the room with Titi, as he figured out what had just happened and that he was going to take care of it right then and there.

The next thing I heard was a lot of yelling and screaming, and some popping like someone was getting punched in the face. Almost like those old Batman movies where they would put words on the screen for expressing the actions being done. I heard Tio tell him to get out of the house and not to come back. He called him a sick fuck, saying, "She's just a little girl."

I can remember Titi holding me tight. I was shaking and that was the first time I can ever remember her holding me so close, like a mother protecting her young. I really was scared and thankful that she was there.

It suddenly got quiet and Tio came into the room to see how I was doing. I had calmed down and was feeling safe. All I thought about at that time was that my tio had come to the rescue and at that moment was where I felt a connection to my tio and Tia like never before.

He apologized to me repeatedly, and told me it was wrong what he had done and never to let any man do that to me no matter whom he was. He said he was proud of me. But no sooner did he say that, he begged me not to tell anyone. That he took care of it and no one needed to know. I was traumatized enough. How could I tell anyone anyway and have to relive it?

I soon fell asleep in Tia's bed and when I woke up Titi and Tio were talking in the living room. I swear it was about what happened because Titi said she never wanted him back in the house again. I think they still were both afraid I would tell someone because when they saw me coming, the mood changed and they started paying extra attention to me.

On our way home that night from the city, I was feeling empty and dirty. I had already taken a shower, but when I got home I took another shower, trying to wash the dirty feeling away. I felt him all over me. I felt his growth. That's all I kept thinking about, and the dirtier I felt I got.

After Mami yelled at me to get out of the shower already because I was going to shrivel up, I got out and put on my PJs. I sat down to watch TV for a little while, some Sunday Disney special. Mami asked if I was feeling okay and I told her I wasn't feeling that great. She took my temperature but nothing. She thought I was trying to get out of school the next day. If she only knew, I thought to myself. She sat down next to me and she said she did notice me being a bit quiet earlier. I told her I was just tired from playing with the baby too much and that babies are a handful. I was trying to throw my mother off because I didn't want to think about it anymore and have to explain what had happened. I couldn't go through it again.

The next day when I went to school, I tried to act as normal as possible. I tried not to think about it and for a while it worked. The feeling of ugliness, disgust, and the disbelief went away for a while. I didn't, couldn't even tell my best friend what happened. What would she think of me?

Later that week when I was coming home from school, it became overwhelming. I had left my house key inside the house in my room. I cried uncontrollably. I felt so sick inside and I couldn't tell anyone. No one. I was so upset that I put my fist through one of the glass panels of the kitchen door. I cried even harder as I knew Papi was going to be mad and possibly kill me. Oh wait, that may be a good thing.

Blood was everywhere, but I managed to pull myself together. I cleaned up the mess, as now I could get into the house, put a Band-Aid on and all was good.

Well, at least physically. Mentally was a different story…

Chapter 5

"For you created my inmost being; you knit me
together in my mother's womb."
– Psalm 139:13 (NIV)

She cried with me. I felt like she really understood what I was feeling. The agony I was going through.

I was scared to death, ashamed of this situation that I was in. I didn't want to do this. I hated the idea. I told the counselor that, and she shared her story with me and what she had done and how she came out of it.

I knew when I walked into this place that it wasn't for me. So many people. So many different faces and so many different reasons.

We had to go through the back of the building as there were groups of people in the front picketing. I think that is where I got really anxious, nervous and scared. Seeing all those people fighting. My body felt like it was going limp.

Mami and my cousin were talking to me, but I couldn't hear them. It was like a Charlie Brown movie. Words were coming out like sounds.

I tried not to think about it, but the more I fought it, the more it came to the forefront of my brain. It was all I could think about.

When we finally walked in, Mami went to the counter to check me in and my cousin and I went to sit down. The movie with Dustin Hoffman, *Tootsie,* was on. It was pretty funny but not that day. I couldn't even crack a smile if you paid me.

It felt as if hours instead of minutes had gone by before I heard my name called. I got up to walk into the back offices when I saw her walking toward me. She led me into this room where she could inform me of what was going to happen and basically talk. She asked me if I knew what was going to happen, if I understood why I was there and how I was feeling about it all. I told her yes, or shall I say basically nodded as she went ahead and explained what was going to happen anyway. I just began to cry and cry and cry.

I started telling her how I got there, why I was there and why I didn't want to be there and that I was only there because my parents made me come. I actually was hoping it was going to be too late.

She said the next step was going to be an examination, but when we went to the exam room they were all occupied so I had to wait again and she sent me back out to the waiting room with all the other lost children.

I was called again, but this time by a nurse and she walked me into the exam room. Next thing I know my legs were in stirrups and the doctor began to give me a pelvic exam. He told me they were going to put me to sleep, but before that I would feel a sharp pain inside me. Out like a light.

I woke up in recovery in a bed with curtain walls. I felt like I was in some third world country hospital. The space was no bigger than a closet. A nurse came up to me to check on me and asked me how I was. I couldn't answer her as I was still a bit groggy. She said that was normal, but she would let Mami know I was ready to go. Go? Go where?

I began to get dressed and my cousin helped me while Mami went to get the car. They both helped me get into the car and I slept all the way home. One and half hour drive. When we got home, Mami sent me straight to bed. Papi was home doing work and he ran up from the basement.

"Is it done?" he asked.

"Yes," I said and went to my room where I spend the rest of the day and night.

The next day everyone left to go to work and I was home alone. How I cried. For me, for my baby, for him, for us. I called him and he asked how I was. I don't remember what I told him, but he said he was sorry and that he loved me. It was so hard to comprehend at that time as I didn't understand why he didn't come to save me. He didn't stop it from happening. He wasn't my knight in shining armor that I needed so desperately the day before.

I felt such emptiness, such a loss and such a hurt that seemed almost unbearable. I could barely speak

In my room, I had this doll that I used to play with as a child and I just carried it around all day. I think it was a girl. I wanted it to be a girl. I had already picked out her name and my doll became my baby.

No one understood what I had just gone through. No one to talk to about it. There were even times that mis padres would later make comments about it that were so hurtful. "I don't want no zebra babies." Or somebody's cousin had the same situation and the mother had the girl's tubes tied and cut so she would never have children for embarrassing the family for getting pregnant in the first place. Things I really didn't need to hear or want to hear. Things that often times were more hurtful than the act itself.

I thought to myself, *Why didn't I stand up for myself, my baby?* It was the shame of embarrassing my family that kept me from saying anything. But I should have fought for that unborn child!

While the embarrassment for my family was gone, the pain that I endured silently wasn't.

Chapter 6

"On that day you will know that I am in my
Father, and you in me, and I in you."
—John 14:20 (NRSVCE)

I announced my name and that was it. The woman standing next to me said, "What? That is all you're going to say?" I nodded yes. She then proceeded to say her name and why she was here. As I stood up there listening to all these women, I thought to myself, *Why am I here? I've done so many of these things that I could run circles around these women. I bought a T-shirt at that drama store and the pants to go with it at another and the accessories at another.*

I don't need this. How do I get out of here? I know no one here and don't care to.

"I think this is not for me. I took someone else's spot who needed to be here," I told my friend.

She said, "Girl, just enjoy the weekend. How often do you get to spend time away from home without the kids?"

Enough, I thought to myself. I begged her to take me home. She asked me to just spend the night. It was already late and maybe I'd feel differently in the morning.

Well, I wasn't going home that night and why would I feel differently in the morning? How was sleeping in a room with three other women I didn't know, on a top bunk bed, freezing my ass off, going to make me feel any different? My boys were home alone. Well, they were already teenagers and I had someone looking out for them, but still I'm their mother. At least I had kept my phone, so I'd know if something was up or I could at least check in.

As I listened to the talks that morning, I still didn't get it and I was asked what I hoped to get out of the weekend. This retreat? Well, my first thought was out of here, but I said, "I don't know; don't really have any issues pending." (Yeah right). I didn't have any issues and I had already gone through half the crap these women had already gone through or were going through and I was in a good place.

As we sat in our circle drinking wine and sharing our stories, I started opening up and sharing who and what I had gone through. Since I couldn't go home, I had made up my mind to be plain stubborn and stay to myself. I wasn't going to talk, give my opinion, etc. I did enjoy the pampering, however, that I was receiving so I let that happen, but it wasn't until we were in our private, small group that I realized how broken these women were and how broken I truly was and had been. I never saw myself that way until that very moment and how much God had carried me through. Don't get me wrong, I believed in God, loved and adored him. Raised my boys in the Catholic faith (after my divorce), they did RCIA, was baptized, confirmed and in Youth Group. So no doubt I knew God, but I never gave him credit for helping me through all those dark days, those hours of soaked pillow tears, the agonies of the heart.

As I listened more throughout the day, my heart softened, and my mind loosened and I sank into the abyss of God's calling and love.

That evening we had an activity where we were called to look deep into our souls to see how we had treated others around us. (Well, I knew then I probably was going straight to hell in a hand basket with a handle.) How we treated members of our family, etc., and my boys came immediately to mind. The tears instantly ran down my face. Did I appreciate my beautiful boys? Had I shown them enough love? Had I been there when they really needed me? All these questions came to mind within seconds, but then God spoke to me. In the depths of my soul when I thought of the child I didn't have. He forgave me.

I went to confession and told the priest all my sins, and especially about the child I didn't have and how I wanted to be such a better mother to the children I did have. The priest said I had been forgiven, but I must forgive myself as well. Well that was a doozy as I thought I had, but the spirit had moved me and I saw things differently. My roommates and I talked ourselves to sleep that night and a special bond formed in that room that night. We would never be the same. The same women, the same mothers, same wives or even the same friends. We were given another chance. WE had cleansed our souls and I, for one, felt such a high. A high for God.

As we prepared ourselves to go home the next morning, I remembered a conversation I had with my youngest son the day before. (I snuck a phone call home to my boys during a break). He was a bit upset with me and said, "Mom, you're not supposed to have your phone. We are fine, this weekend is for you. Don't worry about us." That's when I knew that God was in control. I also began to understand the true treasures that were given to me by God. Those were my children.

When we arrived at the church, I felt a sudden peace, along with an instant concern of what next? How do I keep this fire in my heart burning? But when I saw my boys' faces, I knew then the fire wouldn't die.

"Mom, over here!" They were all dressed up and had flowers for me, along with their big grins. They had gone to a Lifeteen retreat months before and loved it. So they knew how I would feel.

I told them how much I loved them and that we were so blessed. As we drove home, I remember my sons saying to me, when they left their retreat, that things looked brighter and different, and asked me why that was. I said, "Because God has come into your heart." That is the same feeling I had that bright and colorful Sunday afternoon.

Chapter 7

"God is our refuge and strength."
—Psalm 46:1 (NRSVACE)

hat are you saying? What do you mean?"

"Relax, calm down."

"I'm not crazy. I'm not! You're crazy!"

"You need to take time off from work. You can't go back right now. I'm going to have you take a leave of absence for at least two months."

"What? I can't do that."

"You have no choice. I'm also referring you to a psychiatrist. You need to see him ASAP."

"What about my job? I have to work."

"You are suffering from an anxiety attack right now and it sounds like it's not the first one. From what you're telling me, and how you are right now, you are also suffering from depression. I'm also suggesting you be hospitalized for a while."

"No, no. I can't do that. My boys. They are too small to understand. I'll do anything else, but not a hospital."

The doctor provided me information to give to my job and he also called to let them know I would need to be on leave for a while. He prescribed some anti-depressants and I was put on suicide watch, which meant I would get a call every two hours. I was then assigned a psychiatrist that I had to see two times a week.

This was serious, I thought to myself. I had no idea what had happened to me. It hit me like a ton of bricks. I was only in my mid-twenties. This doesn't happen to women this age. How the heck would I know anyway? I never met anyone who suffered from anxiety depression before. Hell, I don't even know how you get it.

When I told Lynn what was happening and what I needed to do, he of course was NO SUPPORT. "What about your job? Who is going to take care of the kids, if you go into the hospital?"

After I told him I wasn't going into the hospital and explained that I would get worker's comp—sixty-six percent of my salary while out on leave and the kids could stay home with me. He seemed to calm down a bit. He was still an ass. He wasn't supportive at all. You would've thought I had the plague. I couldn't tell anyone. I had to act normal around everyone and just say I was on vacation or the kids were sick, etc. "BS" as far as I was concerned. In the meantime, I slept, I cried, I dreaded getting up and I didn't eat (only good thing about it—losing weight). My only joy during this time was my boys. They would come into my room and wake me up, and I indulged them with all my time. That was the only thing that kept me sane and, of course, the phone calls every two hours. They were like mini-therapy sessions. "Good Morning. How are you feeling today? Anything you want to talk about?" Often times no, because I had started my therapy and I was involved with my boys so I was able to maintain. One time I was in the bathroom and my oldest answered the phone. Oh my God. I thought the fire department, rescue squad and the police department was going to bust through my door any minute.

My oldest had said I was in the bathroom and the doctor must have asked how long I had been in there and he said, "I don't know, a little bit," which is nothing in laymen's terms, but not to the psychiatrist. He asked my son if he could talk to me and he said "She's in the bathroom." When I finally heard my son on the phone talking, I asked who he was talking to and he said he didn't know. I looked at the time and I grabbed the phone. "I'm here, I'm here," I said.

"Good, I was just about to send help." That's all I needed—talk about anxiety. I didn't want my kids witnessing that craziness.

I started my twice a week therapy with an older psychiatrist. I felt like I had to travel to Timbuktu to see him and I had no one to watch my boys during my sessions, so I had a portable TV that I brought with me, so they could sit and wait for Mommy. I explained how important it was for them to let Mommy do what she needed to do and a special treat would come after we left if they behaved. Ironically enough, they were always really good.

The psychiatrist explained to me what I was suffering from, but now we had to figure out why this happened and how to fix it, but we had to go back to the beginning. In the meantime, we started with the now.

I talked about my job, my marriage, my family life, my upbringing, my parents, etc. I don't even remember how much or how often I cried, but I suffered a headache every time I left his office. I was falling apart into a thousand pieces. I felt like a jigsaw puzzle shaken in its box and waiting to be put back together, which meant I couldn't do it alone.

After my first two visits, the doctor thought it was okay to take me off suicide watch as he felt I was no longer a threat to myself or anyone else for that matter. That what really stabilized me were my boys and he saw how much I loved them by the way I hugged them and interacted with them. But as they may not call every two hours, they may call on days I didn't see him for at least the next two weeks.

A few weeks later, Ray, one of Lynn's friends, came by the house for dinner. Lynn was starting a fire as we digested our food, and Ray starting asking me about work and I said I was on leave for a while.

"Oh, why? I didn't know."

I said I was suffering from anxiety attacks. What did I say that for?

Lynn immediately jumped in and got upset and said, "Yeah, man, she's been acting like she's crazy and they gave her some time off from work. She just didn't want to work. Can you believe that? Maybe, I should do something like that and see what happens."

I really was going to go crazy. I got so angry that I started to cry; cry from anger. Ray looked at me and I could tell he felt sorry for me. I just walked out and went straight to my room. As I was going up the stairs to my room, I heard Ray tell Lynn that he shouldn't have done that and it wasn't right. Lynn, of course, ignored him and started bitching about money, etc. *Selfish bastard*, I thought. Then I knew I was getting better. I was getting my strength back.

Lynn continued to do things to agitate me and do things to prevent me from getting better. It was like he wanted me to stay submissive and act like all was fine, but through my therapy, my strength started building.

One day, Lynn decided to take my car and left me with his dad's old Cadillac. It was having problems and he didn't want to drive it so far to work every day, so he would take my car and leave me his, since I was only going to be home. The boys were always with me so you'd think he'd leave the better car with me in case of an emergency, but nope, he only thought of himself. But often more than not, he wasn't coming home or came home late or would be gone all weekend. On this particular Friday, I called him to see what time he would be home because I knew he was planning something. Of course, he didn't know. So I packed up all his clothes, dumped them in the trunk of his car and wherever there was space, I packed the boys up. Since I knew where the car was parked, I took my spare keys and off we went to his job. I moved my car, put the boys in the car and put his car with his shit in his spot. I wish I could've been a fly when he came out looking for my car and saw his. What a Kodak moment that would've been, and on top of that find all his stuff thrown in the trunk of his car. I left with a big ass grin on my face. The boys asked what I was doing and just told them we were playing musical cars and that Daddy had somewhere to go and didn't know what he wanted to wear and didn't know when he'd be back. So we headed back home. I parked the car somewhere not so obvious in the event he tried to come take my car back, and made the boys play in the backyard in case he did a drive-by. I sat and waited by the phone, because I just knew he was going to be fired up. As I suspected, he called and I just let the answering machine get it. Once I heard his voice over the machine, I would delete the message, just to keep my sanity.

I was feeling good. Feeling stronger. I noticed I was sleeping better, wasn't reading books to escape anymore or trying to sleep all day. I actually was enjoying reading to the kids, doing arts and crafts with them, teaching them Spanish and teaching them to dance Salsa. We had fun and my insides were warming up; I could see the rays of light through the gray again. I started living again. Sunday came and he came by the house. I was outside with the boys. Damn, I had let my guard down. We shouldn't have been out front with the neighborhood kids, but when the boys saw him, they were so happy to see him and with their smiles I put a half-ass smile on my face so the boys didn't notice. He asked to talk to me as I didn't follow him and the boys inside. I stayed outside talking to one of the neighbors when he called me inside. We talked and I listened, he wanted to come back home and as he emptied his own car, I cooked dinner. We made love that night, but deep inside me, I knew things wouldn't change for long.

A few weeks later, I went back to work with a modified schedule. I still had to go to therapy so I went through our EAP program at work and was still on anti-depressants, but I slowly weaned myself off them as it affected the way I worked.

As expected, things went back to the way they were. Of course, not all at once, but little by little and by that summer, I decided something had to change.

Chapter 8

"...let us love one another. ⁶ And this is love, that we walk according to his commandments; this is the commandment just as you have heard it from the beginning— you must walk in it."
—2 John 1:5-6 (NRSVCE)

Jay was just a few months old, but I had to leave. I couldn't take it anymore. My cousin drove down from Jersey to pick me up so I could stay with her. She was one of the only few members of my family that spoke to me regularly.

I had to rebuild Jays crib and I stayed in her brother's old room. Her brother and another friend of theirs were staying in their parents' old house. Titi and Tio had moved to South Florida to retire and my cousins kept the house in Jersey. It was a small room, but my cousin had rearranged everything, so she was in her parents' old room and my other cousin moved into her old room and their friend stayed in the basement. It actually was pretty cool and it worked out well. I was twenty-one, with a baby, separated, no job and feeling like a hippie. My parents lived five minutes away and I hadn't spoken to them in two years. My cousin encouraged me to call after a week of being with her. They knew I had had a baby, but had never seen him, so I took Jay to see them. Jay was such a perfect baby. He looked just like the Gerber baby you would see on the cereal boxes. He was beautiful with a perfect round head. My mother adored him, my father did, too, but I could still feel their disappointment piercing through me. We had general conversation at first. Nothing deep. When my brother came over, I was so excited to see him. We talked and talked, and he fell in love with Jay, too. He was an uncle.

As time passed, I continued to stay with my cousin and my husband-to-be as we were just engaged at the time.

He would call every so often. He would send money, but nothing was getting resolved.

One day, we were all watching the movie *Dirty Dancing* with Patrick Swayze and I got up and tried to do some of the moves with Miguel, our other housemate (because he was such a good dancer). Our eyes met and I think that is when the chemistry began. We tried to fight it at first. We both were wounded and not sure if what we felt was real or not. We would avoid each other or not look at each other, but I think my cousin caught on and she had a bit of a crush on Miguel and she told me to be careful and that he's not the one for me.

He would help me with Jay from time to time. He was really good with him and with me.

One afternoon, I needed to go and apply for aid, so he offered to take me. After the appointment we got something to eat. He tells me his story. He fell in love with this girl and they had a baby girl. The mother of his girlfriend didn't like him because he was Puerto Rican and the girl started to believe the things her mother would tell her. They fought a lot and she took their daughter and moved to Colorado. All the way on the other side of the country. He was devastated. He often sent money and would call, but his heart really ached for his daughter. He told me he really enjoyed spending time with Jay because he reminded him of his baby girl and the times he had spent with her when she was that small. Jay just giggled at him like he knew he was talking about him.

We formed a special bond and kissed for the first time. I told him what my cousin said and he told me he knew something was up. We'd have to keep our feelings to ourselves and not be obvious. So we did just that. Kept it casual. Didn't make any extra efforts to run into each other. It wasn't that difficult since she had to work early and I was home most of the time, and Miguel's work schedule was sporadic. The first time we made love it was like the movie, *Dirty Dancing*, and that's exactly how we felt. Our relationship could not be known by anyone and, in a sense, it kept it exciting. We really enjoyed each other and we comforted each other through our pains and suffering from our significant others. I think that was the only time we were able to console each other in front of everyone because my cousins knew we were going through the same thing at the very same time. We never told each other we loved each other. That wasn't really what it was about, but we genuinely cared for each other in a way no one else could understand. Lynn called one day and said he missed me and the baby. He wanted his family back and enough was enough, he was coming to get us. Two months had passed by. I had to tell Miguel. I knew he was going to be upset.

"I can't believe you're going back to him. He's not right for you."

"He is Jay's father and I have to try. I do still love him, at least I think I do, but that doesn't change the way I feel about you, and I don't regret anything we did together."

It was true. We were two lost souls that helped each other to get ourselves together again. We supported each other during a difficult time in our life and there was nothing to be ashamed of and if nothing else he would always hold a special place in my heart.

Of course, I heard the same disappointment from my cousins, my parents and my brother.

That Saturday afternoon, Lynn showed up to take us home. He packed up the car and he waited in the car as I said my goodbyes.

Miguel came up to give Jay a hug. The way he hugged Jay goodbye broke my heart and tears formed in my eyes. He looked at me as he hugged Jay and I had to turn away. I thanked my cousins for everything they did for me and that I loved them very much. As I approached Miguel and gave him a hug, he thanked me for showing him how to be a man and to love again, and that he would never forget me. I gave him a kiss on the cheek and stroked the side of his face and left.

As I got in the car, I looked toward the house, waving goodbye with tears in my eyes. Lynn asked me what that was all about and I said that he had lost his daughter and he grew a bound with Jay and I felt sorry for him. Lynn didn't say a word after that. I never did tell him how exactly Miguel lost his daughter and let him believed that she had died.

As we drove out of my cousin's community, he talked about all the changes he had made. I didn't hear a word he had said. All I thought about was what Miguel had said. I never saw or heard from him again, but every time I see the movie *Dirty Dancing*, I think of Miguel and the special friendship we formed, and only imagined him driving off in his car to a better place.

Chapter 9

*"What I say to you in the dark, tell in the light; and what
you hear whispered, proclaim from the housetops."*
—Matthew 10:27 (NRSVCE)

Okay, we're going to let you drive your car to the
station, park it and then you have to get in the squad
car."

"What about my boys? Can I take them to my friend's
house until their father can pick them up?"

"Yes, we'll follow you."

I was a hot mess. I didn't know what to do. I had to
stop crying so as not to upset the boys. I had already called
my parents in complete hysteria.

I was so shocked when they approached me that I thought I had been dreaming.

A bench warrant for my arrest for failure to appear in court for a traffic citation was put out on me. I explained to the cops that I had taken care of the ticket and that my license had been reinstated. They didn't want to hear it. Well, at least one of the cops didn't want to hear it. That one cop was pretty nice and was willing to work with me. I tried to call Lynn, but he didn't answer. I had no idea where he was, which was no surprise to me. We hadn't long broken up so he was free as a bird as far as he was concerned. I took the boys to my girlfriend's house, gave her Lynn's number and my parents'. I told her to keep trying Lynn until she got him to get the boys. I explained to the boys that Mommy had to go to a meeting with the police officers and Daddy would pick them up soon. I hugged them as if it would be the last time and told them I loved them.

As I was driving up to the house after work, I saw two cops sitting in their car in front of the house. I thought it strange for cops to just be sitting there, but thought nothing else of it until they came knocking at my door.

They asked if I was who I was and I said yes, as my heart raced. When they told me they were here to arrest me, the first thought that came to mind, after I almost fell to my knees, was how many tickets had that son of a bitch not paid for on top of what happened when I got pulled over.

It was mid-October when I and a few of my friends were on our way to a seminar on Leadership for Latin Americans. It was an early Saturday morning. I was driving and had picked up Jose and Carlos. I missed the exit by two feet, and as I backed up, a cop pulled me over. He informed me that my license had been suspended and I couldn't drive, but that one of the other guys could drive. He then informed me that I had to pay the tickets plus the one he gave me and get my license reinstated. Oh wow. Great, another expense and crazy thing to add to my already crazy life. My hopefully soon-to-be ex-husband continued to haunt me anyway he could. The cop informed me that my license was suspended for unpaid tickets on the car that were at least eighteen months old. My husband never paid the tickets on the car—parking tickets no less—and of course, since we were split up it became my responsibility to pay them since the car was in my name and I had to appear in court. Great!

Late November, mi abuela died. The funeral was in New York and my husband had given me his car to drive up since my car was acting up and I was taking the boys. Sure he wanted something for being nice, but I didn't care at the time since I had a funeral to worry about. As I was coming back from the funeral, I was side swiped on the driver's side. *Oh Jesus, I'll never hear the end of it*, I thought. The BMW was smashed in and since we were in Jersey, a no-fault state, our insurance had to pay for it because, of course, the other driver didn't want to take responsibility and came up with some story, etc. Anyway, no one got a ticket; we just had to figure it out on the insurance side. That conversation with my husband was handled by Papi because I just knew it wasn't going to be a good one, so Papi took it on and an agreement was met.

In the meantime, my court hearing was the day of my abuela's funeral and I had informed the courts that I was out of town due to the death of a family member. They would inform me of a new court date.

Well, maybe I should have called to follow-up or maybe I just never thought about it again, but I really wished I had.

As I parked my car, one of the cops walked over to handcuff me and put me in the back of the squad car, but the nice cop didn't think it was necessary since I had followed through with everything asked and didn't think I'd pull anything.

As I walked into the jail, they had open cells filled with tons of men, gawking at me, taunting me and saying all kinds of vulgarities and things I had never even heard. I started freaking out. I couldn't believe I was in this mess. I kept screaming to myself, *Wake up, Wake up. This has got to be a nightmare. This can't be happening.*

As they took my fingerprints, photo and all my personal belongings, I began to cry. A female officer led me to my cell and then shoved me in welcoming me to my HELL.

There were screams coming diagonally across from my cell. I heard the guards say she was a Hispanic woman who attempted to stab her man for cheating. She didn't speak English and they said, "She probably just came over the border." They were trying to talk broken Spanish to her, but it wasn't calming her down. In fact, it made her angrier. She would get even crazier and irrational. She was spitting, pissing and crapping all over the cell and when they tried to go in, she'd go into attack mode and three guards would have to go in and hold her down. She would throw food at them and start screaming. At that point, I just wanted to die. I was scared to death. Here I was in a cell the size of my closet with just a sink, a toilet and a bed that felt like a sack of lumpy potatoes rather than a mattress. All I could do was cry and cry and cry. Finally a guard showed up to allow me my one phone call and I called my girlfriend who had my boys. She told me she got a hold of their father and he was coming to pick them up. I only had a few minutes and the guard kicked me off. She took me to my cell and more crying. I was in such a dark place, wondering why and how did I get here. I couldn't think straight and the woman across the hall didn't help with her constant screaming and the guards yelling at her to shut up. With that thought, I cried even harder. My head was feeling like it was about to explode from a headache coming on. All of a sudden I heard a woman's voice from another cell. The walls were made of cement and concrete; how was I able to hear anyone or they hear me? Then I thought, *Well, I can hear crazy across the hall.* She kept telling me, "It's going to be okay. Stop crying and they'll let you use the phone again." I instantly stopped the hard crying and kept it down to a whimper.

"What's your name?" she asked.

So I told her and she told me hers.

"This is your first time in a jail, isn't it?"

"Yeah." Between my tears I answered her questions.

She asked about me and what happened, and then she asked if I had kids and that made me cry harder all over again. So she calmed me down and told me she had been there for a week. She hadn't been able to get an arraignment for some reason. *A week!"* I thought, *I'll die. I can't be in here a week.* She then started to fill me in on what to expect the next day. To stay calm, don't give the guards a hard time and just do what they tell me to do. Try to relax. It was lights out and she talked me to sleep. My head was hurting so badly from all the crying that I couldn't do anything else. My body just went limp and while I tossed and turned all night, I knew a stranger on the other side was there for me. Just knowing that kept me calm and allowed me to fall sleep.

The cell door opened. "Get up and get ready to go," the guard said.

"Where am I going?" I asked, dreading what she would say.

"You're getting out of here."

I couldn't believe it! How?

The woman behind the wall said, "I told you. Good luck!"

As I washed my face from all the tears and makeup smeared all over my face, I put my shoes on and walked in disbelief. I walked down the halls, down to get my personal belongings and I noticed a woman behind the counter. A pretty, petite, older, African American woman with such a gentle voice. The door to the free world opened and they told me I was free to leave and handed me my court papers. The woman walked up to me and introduced herself. She had bailed me out. She was the mother to my brother's friend and she was here to help. I just hugged her and cried. She walked me to my car as I told her the police allowed me to drive my own car down the night before. She told me my parents were waiting on my call, to go straight home and drive safely. She added that my parents took care of my job, and she would call me later to see how I was doing.

I got in my car and drove straight home. I got directly in the shower and washed from head to toe. I stood in the shower, crying what seemed like hours or until the water got too cold to stand in the shower anymore. I was so grateful to be home.

"Mami, it's me."

"Oh my God, my poor baby", she cried.

We both began crying over the phone.

"How are you?" she asked, followed by her being sorry that she didn't live closer and she didn't know what to do

I told her everything from the crazy lady across the hall to the mystery woman behind the wall to my ultimate fears. We cried some more and I thanked Mami and Papi for finding the lady who helped me. My brother called thereafter and was thankful I was okay. He was so worried about me.

My ex-husband was my next call and he, of course, said he tried to find out where I was and couldn't. He wanted to help.

"Really?" I said. "My parents found me and they don't even live in the same state. How is it you couldn't find me?"

He didn't answer.

I asked about the boys and he said he would bring them home soon. I needed to sleep. I was exhausted. I felt I was living in a horror movie and was just waking up from it. Eighteen hours of fear, disgust, and demeaning felt like eighteen years.

"Mommie," my boys cried. I ran to them as I received bunches of hugs and kisses. I was home. Everything was going to be all right.

A few weeks later, I had to appear in court. My parents were there along with the pretty, petite woman who bailed me out. I was placed on probation for six months, but once I complied, all charges were dropped.

All this behind unpaid parking tickets…

Chapter 10

"*Although he causes grief, he will have compassion*
according to the abundance of his steadfast love."
—Lamentations 3:32 (NRSVCE)

I started crying. I don't know what exactly came over me, but I just started crying. He was on top of me looking down at me. It wasn't like I didn't want him, otherwise I wouldn't have been here and my body had been craving it for some time now. It had been so long, but I hadn't been with another man since I married my husband. It was strange being with someone else. He stopped and he asked me what was wrong. As I tried to explain to him what I was feeling he listened, but I didn't get the impression that he understood. I felt like a girl who had just lost her virginity. Well, that was not the case, since I'd already had two kids. I couldn't go on so I got up, got dressed and left. He tried to console me and convinced me to stay. I just couldn't. He called again from time to time and finally after a few days later we tried it again and I was fine. He was a younger guy and since I had been married I was quite prudish. I didn't like any crazy stuff or stunts shall I say. Certain positions just weren't happening and Hell if I liked someone dripping all over me with their sweat. That was it! Not happening. After a few times with him, I stopped taking his calls and eventually he stopped calling.

A few months later, a girlfriend of mine convinced me to go on the personals. She told me she had met quite a few professional men — doctors, lawyers, etc. and thought I should try it out. I was quite reluctant. I didn't care how professional they were, I wasn't into meeting a whole bunch of crazy guys that were just interested in one thing. Plus what would I say in the ad. I didn't know the first thing to say about myself or even what I was looking for in a guy. Well, she decided to write it for me and placed the ad out herself. I thought I would die. But she convinced me it was safe way to meet guys and they would just respond via telephone to a number designated for me. No personal data would be shared. So when it was time to meet the guys, we developed a system of asking them to take us to lunch. When I had a date she woud go ahead of me to the lobby to check the guys out and then report back to me and I did the same for her. The lobby guard even got involved. She would start to call one of us and then report: good, bad, or maybe. It was kind of fun for a while, but some of the guys were just not worth the trouble to go downstairs.

Sammy was different. He sounded really good over the phone and we had a lot in common. We finally decided to meet after talking on the phone for quite some time.

I invited Sammy to my house one Sunday afternoon and the moment I saw him I was like, Uh ah, no way. He looked too much like my uncle. I even told him that. He laughed; he really thought it was funny. I didn't!

We spent the afternoon talking and my boys had come in from playing outside and I introduced them to Sammy. He had a way with kids and they seemed to get along. He stayed for dinner and not too long after went home.

We spoke for days and he began to grow on me. Soon after, we got into a serious relationship.

He was half black and half Puerto Rican just like my kids. That was the first thing I liked about him. He was a hard worker and a jack of all trades. Seemed he had done a little bit of everything and really cared for his family. He really became a great support for me and my boys, especially during the difficult times in dealing with my soon to be ex-husband. I could always count on him to tell me how it was.

So much so, we had a huge fight. We didn't fight often but when we did, watch out! And this fight was over a gown I was to wear to an Awards Banquet. My Awards Banquet.

I was to receive the YOUNG ENTREPRENEUR OF THE YEAR award from a local Hispanic Chamber of Commerce. I was so excited and my girlfriend and I went shopping for the gown. We spent the whole day looking for the right dress. When I saw it, I knew. I just knew it was the one. It was beautiful. Off white, lace down the back, flowed in the front. Perfect. It needed some resizing, but my girlfriend knew where to go, a seamstress to get the dress refitted to my body. Perfect. Grabbed it off the shelf and headed straight to the seamstress.

That following weekend, one of our old high school friends was coming down for a visit, so Sammy and I went to my girlfriend's house to see her. My girlfriend and I began discussing the awards dinner and then described the gown and how it looked, etc. I noticed Sammy listening (since he was taking me to the awards dinner), he made this funny face but I didn't pay attention to him or think anything of it.

A week later, I was attending a going away party for my boss in Maryland, not too far from where Sammy lived. Sammy paged me to call him. I thought it kind of odd for him to page me since he knew where I was and he had paged me several times, so I figured I'd better call him right away. "Hey baby," he says. "How's the party?" "Nice" I said. "What's wrong? You paged me a few times." "Oh, nothing really. Listen, I want you to stop by here before you go home to try on some dresses that my sister has." I was shocked that he pulled me away from a party to talk about some dresses. "Sammy, why are you calling me now about some dresses? Dresses for what?"

"I don't like the dress you have for the Awards Dinner." He said. "It sounded kind of old fashioned and I think my sister would have some better dresses for you."

Well, I know his sister and forgive me, but there was no way I was going to fit into his big booty sisters dresses. I could only imagine what she gave him for me to try on.

"Sammy, are you serious? You haven't even seen the dress. Are you trying to tell me I don't have any taste in clothes? What is wrong with you?" I was so offended, we got into a screaming match over the phone and I hung up on him.

I didn't answer his calls for two days. I was livid. Who the hell did he think he was telling me how to dress? After all, he hadn't even seen the dress yet. That's it. Bad enough my ex-husband always tried to control what I wore, where I went, etc. I'll be damned if this guy was going to do the same. Oh, HELL NO!

It was Sunday afternoon and the boys and I went to my office to get some work done and to really avoid hearing the phone ring. We came home early that afternoon and the boys went outside to play. As I was talking to my girlfriend and bitching about Sammy, a knock was at the door. It was Sammy, he wanted to talk. So I got off the phone and we talked.

"I've been trying to call you for two days." He said. "Yea, and?" I said. "Well, when you didn't answer my calls, I decided to come by."

I was so pissed off. I had already gotten a back-up to take me to the Awards dinner. "How dare you assume I have bad taste in picking out evening gowns." and I added that why would I wear something that not only embarrassed him, but myself as well. Let us not forget I'm the one receiving the award. I told him I was not going to try on any other dressings and if he didn't want to take me to the dinner then so be it. We talked it out and we decided he should see the dress before any more discussion was had about it.

Three days later, I went to pick up the dress from the seamstress. "Sammy, I have the dress—you may come and see it if you want." "Ok, I'm on my way" he says.

When he arrived an hour later, I was in the mist of cleaning house. I had hung the dress in my laundry room away from everything so it wouldn't get wrinkled. The dinner was in two days. He came in and we chit-chatted for a while and then he said, "Ok, let's see the dress." Reluctantly, I went to the laundry room to get the dress.

"Sammy, I swear, one bad thing, you're out of here." So, I pulled the dress out from behind me and he started to laugh. I lost it. "Get out! Get out! Get out!". "No, no wait. Let me tell you why I'm laughing." While I stood there waiting for him to compose and explain himself, the smoke kept coming from my ears.

"I thought the dress was one of those old-fashioned southern belle things. It's beautiful, the dress." "What? What made you think it was that type of dress? Like something from Gone with the Wind? Are you crazy?" I asked him again, what he was thinking because I had no clue. I even said, either you have not been to a lot of awards dinners or you've gone with old ladies. We laughed about it afterwards and thought about the stupid fight we had over the dress. That was the first real fight we had and with several more to come. In the three years that we dated, we broke up and got back together three times.

However, our love affair was very special. He took the young, frightened, timid girl out and helped make me a strong, positive and independent woman. He encouraged me to start my own business so I can be home with my boys. He helped me get my own business consulting firm started. I even was able to teach Spanish in my sons school on the part-time basis, coach little league baseball, take my sons to all their after school activities and enjoy holidays and vacations with them. I had the opportunity to meet First Lady Hilary Rodham Clinton through my business ventures two times.

He was there when I got divorced and every step of the way during the early years of my separation. The good, the bad and the ugly.

He encouraged me to be me. To see my full potential and know that I am somebody worth more than I could have imagined. He helped me build my self-esteem again.

He taught me how to make love. I was such a prude. There only two positions I knew and you couldn't even say the "P" word to me. That was the nastiest word you could say to me. The first time he ever said that to me, I froze and told him to get the hell off me. He just froze in shock. At first he thought I was joking, especially after I told him it was insulting and demeaning to me. I went on and on and on. He got it. A few days later he came back with tons of magazines, Cosmopolitan, Vogue, even Women's Health and Better Homes and Garden (go figure). He said, "Read these. You need to understand how your body works and what is good and bad." Wow, was all I could say. He knew more about a woman's body than I did. The brother did his homework. He was talking to me like I was in a sex education class; he definitely knew what he was talking about. He even knew words that would make you melt and he didn't even have to lay a hand on you. One time I asked him how he knew so much. He said, "Research." And that he did! He researched the hell out of a woman's anatomy.

⊷⩵◉

"I'm sick and you have enough to worry about with the boys. I don't want you taking care of me—it'll be like I was an invalid."

He had Fibro Myalgia. A disease that is a chronic condition that causes pain and stiffness in the muscles. He was in constant pain and was always tired. He at times couldn't even hold a coffee mug or even walk down the street without feeling pain. He was always irritable and times couldn't even finish a conversation.

As we sat and talked in my office, he sat at the edge of the day bed and I sat in front of him on the floor, I tried to reason with him. "Sammy, it doesn't matter. We can get through this." I spent a whole day at Barnes and Noble researching the disease. I told him there were medications and therapy he could go through to help with the symptoms. At the time not a lot of medical information was available to the public. I had never heard of this disease before and I used to work at the University Medical Center. He tried to explain to me that I needed and deserved a full man, not a half a man. The disease made him feel weak and worthless and after all I had been through over the last four years, he couldn't ask me to take care of him. He made up his mind and was going to move to New York for a while. Do some light work and come back and forth for a while until he figured out what he was going to do.

We both cried for hours and held each other for as long as we could. He had become my best friend. He saw me through so many rough times as much as the good times. How could this be happening? But I had to respect his wishes. I had to let him go.

From time to time we would talk and we stayed in touch over the years, but as time would tell it, we lost touch and every so often we find each other and catch up.

I will never forget Sammy, what he did for me and the special bond and love we once shared.

Chapter 11

"*I am weary with my moaning; every night I flood my bed with tears; I drench my couch with my weeping.*"
—*Psalm 6:6 (NRSVCE)*

*I*t had been eight hours. My eyes were blood shot and puffy. My head was splitting open and I couldn't even see well enough to find the aspirin.

I lay on the floor and begged for the pain to stop. My heart ached so much and I felt like a knife had been put through it. But I knew this was coming for a long time.

I had sent the boys to spend the summer with my parents. This was it. We were either going to make it or break it.

The night before my girlfriend had asked me to babysit her baby girl since her and her husband had a date night. I asked Lynn and he was fine with it. In fact he thought it was a good idea to have a baby in the house for a while. Everything seemed to go well that night and when my girlfriend came to pick up the baby with her husband we were having breakfast and just talking and making plans to get together. Soon thereafter they left.

"Where is it? Where is it?" "Where is what?" I asked. That's when the fight began. He had some paperwork he had to do for work and he couldn't find it. I really didn't even know what I was looking for. The fight got even more heated and he said he was done with me and was leaving and not coming back. He was moving in with one of his frat brothers.

That was it. That was what I expected. I knew it. I was hoping he didn't but he did. As I finally lifted my limp body off the floor, I called my sister-in-law and told her, "its over. Lynn left me."

"Woo hoo! Yeah, yeah, yeah. Thank God!"

I couldn't move. I couldn't believe what I was hearing. No sympathy. No "I'm so sorry." Nothing. She was so overjoyed by the news she couldn't contain herself.

"It's the best thing that could have ever happened to you, girl. Trust me on that."

"Are you crazy? My marriage is over." *It's broken, my boys. What will they say? Think? I'm a failure*, I thought. "How could you say you're happy for me?' I cried.

"I know you're hurting, I really do. You're hurting so bad that you feel like you're going to die. That you can't go on. Your life is over. But it's not. This is a new beginning for you and the boys."

She went on to tell me how mad she would get by the way he had treated me over the years. That she tried to tell me so many times, but I wouldn't listen or couldn't understand what she was saying. She knew I loved him and that was why I couldn't see all the shit he would do and say to me.

"He never treated you like a wife, but just a piece of property. You deserve more. Trust me, a year from now this will be like a dream," she said. "The pain you feel now will be nothing in comparison." Then she asked the million-dollar question. "What did your parents say?" I couldn't even fathom calling them. I'd never hear the end of it. She would rub it in my face forever.

"I can't call them," I said.

"They need to know. You can't hide it from them. If you don't call I will."

I froze. "No, no, I'll call. I promise. I'll do it as soon as I hang up with you."

"Okay, then I'm hanging up right now," she said.

I begged her to stay on the line with me a little longer until I got my courage to call my parents. She kept telling me this was a good thing, that I'd be fine. I would see, and to just give it time because time healed all wounds, etc. I cried some more and she was very supportive.

"Okay, it's time to call. I love you and I don't think it's going to be as bad as you think." She hung up.

"Mami?" that was all I could say before she asked me what was wrong. I started crying all over again. I couldn't even talk. I was only able to get out, "Lynn left me." That was it. Nothing else came out after that.

She tried to calm me down and when she was finally able to understand me, she asked me, "When did it happen?" I told her earlier this morning. "And you're just now calling me?"

I told her I just couldn't talk to her then and that the only reason I called now was because my sister-in-law made me call. I had to laugh at just the thought of it.

We talked on the phone for hours with Papi interrupting and Mami explaining what had happened in between. We came up with a plan from this point. I talked to the boys and told them I loved them. I decided to get the boys earlier from my parents' house and was going to fly down there to get them. I don't think I'd be able to drive ten hours by myself in the condition I was in. Hell, I didn't even know if I could make it to work the next day. I was a mess. I finally got off the phone and decided to find the aspirin. My head couldn't hold out anymore. It was at an explosive level of pain. Of course it was, I'd been crying for at least ten hours and hadn't even eaten.

When I finally got off the floor, I was so dizzy, I almost fell over.

What the hell was I going to do? What are the boys going to say? Feel? How would I survive?

I was now a single mother, with two small children who happened to be of mixed races. Black and Puerto Rican. I have just become a statistic.

Chapter 12

"*Hear, my child, your father's instruction, and do not reject your mother's teaching; for they are a fair garland for your head, and pendants for your neck. My child, if sinners entice you, do not consent.*"
—*Proverbs 1:8-10 (NRSVCE)*

I could see from my brother's bedroom window Papi and my brother working in the yard. It broke my heart. Why couldn't they just understand how much we loved each other? Why does a choice like this have to be made? Mami was nowhere to be found. She couldn't handle it. Papi yelled at my brother for something stupid and I knew he was just upset at me and was taking it out on him. I went back to my room to finish packing. Dina would be here soon to pick me up. The plan was for me to spend the night at her house and she would take me to the train station in the morning. I was going to Baltimore to meet the love of my life—Lynn. We were to going to begin our life together there. He got a job there working as an assistant manager for a store and we both were really excited. He had an apartment already just no furniture but he was waiting for me to start to get the house in order. I couldn't wait. Things are going to be great I thought to myself, but I still had a pain in my heart for my family. They hated what I was doing.

⊷⟞⟧⊸

"How did you find out?"

"I am your mother; I know when something is up. I saw you with the suitcase," Mami said. "You were going to just leave and not say anything?"

"I was going to leave a note to explain everything."

"You little bitch!" Mami said. I really knew she was going to be upset and this wasn't the first time she had called me that. I was getting used to it. Mami hadn't been very happy over the last nine months with me, so I knew she was going to blow her top and Papi, well I thought he would kill me.

They tried to talk to me. They had other people talk to me, my cousin who ran off with a guy who nearly ruined her life, etc.

I was going no matter what. I loved him and he loved me and that was the end of that.

"You just don't like him because he's Black." I overheard Mami say one time she didn't want any zebra babies and she had even said it to my face. The fight kept on and on.

Papi said to me, "If you leave this house, you are dead to me. You can never come back."

I felt like one of those old Jewish movies where the daughter tells her family she is marrying outside her religion. The father would condemn his daughter and her name to never be spoken again, rip his shirt and leave. The only difference was Papi didn't rip his shirt.

The fight stopped. I was alone. Mis padres disowned me at that point.

"Are you ready?" Dina asked. I was in the house by myself. Papi and my brother had left to go somewhere and we packed up her car. I walked around the house one last time figuring this was it. I prayed that their hearts would soften and this would eventually not be the end. But I knew my parents, they'd hate me forever.

As a child I had this consistent dream. I would have that same dream every year, sometimes two times a year and never understood it, but today I did.

I was always alone. Sometimes in a room, on a bridge or in an empty building, just crying. I was always looking for my family, but they wouldn't come or I couldn't find them. I would look and look and look and nothing.

All of a sudden another family would appear and they were always dressed in black and they would take me in as one of their own, no questions asked. They loved me and treated me like their own and I would wake up. Always startled at first, but at peace because someone had taken me in to love me. Wow, I thought to myself. I had known all my life this was going to happen. I just didn't understand the dream until that moment. It's funny, because I always sensed that I could somehow predict things, because I could think of something and it would happen. It was the weirdest thing and I never told anyone because I didn't want people to think I was crazy, but I always had a sick sense about things.

As we arrived to Dina's house, I had known that her family would be gone for the weekend, but I suddenly felt a sense of anxiety, nervousness, whatever, just different. We cooked dinner and had a great Italian dinner, she was after all Italian. It was going to be our last meal for a very long time together. We listened to music, ate, drank, laughed and cried. She told me she loved me and thought I was brave. She didn't think she could do what I was doing. Hell, I don't even know I still can. But I did.

The next morning we packed up her car, went to the train station, loaded my stuff onto the train.

We hugged so tight you would've thought our skin had melted together. I hugged her boyfriend goodbye and thanked them for everything and told him to take care of her for me.

As I got to my seat and started to settle in, I looked out the window and they waved to me until I was out of sight.

As the tears ran down my face, I was saying goodbye to a world I once knew and hello to a new world. A new wonderful journey. At least that is what I had hoped for.

Chapter 13

"I have said this to you, so that in me you may have peace.
In the world you face persecution. But take courage;
I have conquered the world!"
—John 16:33 (NRSVCE)

In the words of Celia Cruz, "Mi Espanol no es very good looking," is how I started my talk.

I was a nervous wreck. I had to tell my story to forty-plus women who I had never met before and tell my story in Spanish no less. Wow, what were they thinking when they asked me to tell my story, I thought. It was hard enough to say in English, now I have to do it in Spanish and for the first time ever.

I was humbled and shocked when the women from church asked me to give a talk. I didn't know where or how to begin. My hurts were deep and I was just beginning to heal. So much to say, but in a limited amount of time. I had to write it in English first and then I had to find someone who I could fully trust to translate it into Spanish and keep my story confidential as well as not pass judgment on me for it either. I instantly thought of one person who I felt had such a true heart. When I approached her, she was delighted and honored. She even practiced the speech with me to make sure I hit certain volumes to get the points across.

"This is a broken woman standing in front of you. I have suffered loss, abandonment, abuse and fear. Fear for myself and for my children. I'm a woman who has struggled not just with finances, being a single parent or even being alone, but struggled with being WORTHY! I have often asked myself why I am going through this. Why do my children have to suffer? Why have they seen what they have seen? I have often lied awake being angry at myself for making the choices I have made."

As my speech went deeper into my memories, the pain I suffered resurfaced and became vivid in my mind as if it had just happened yesterday.

"There was a time my ex-husband locked me out of our apartment and I had to sleep in the laundry room because I wanted to go to the movies with a friend. Or the time he slapped me across the face in front of a co-worker because I picked him up late. Or the time he threw a shoe at me while I was doing dishes in the kitchen and just barely missed me.

"During our separation, an agreement was made between our attorneys that he was not to pick up the boys at my place anymore for various incidents that had happened in the past, so we were to meet at the McDonalds' in front of the complex I lived in. On this particular occasion, he was returning the boys to me. Lynn had parked his car right diagonally in front of the drive-thru. The boys were so small then and I was dating Sammy at the time. I was upset because if the boys came running out the car, the car in drive-thru won't be able to see them and they could get hit. Sammy got out of the car before I did and started walking towards Lynn's car. My seat belt was giving me problems so it took me a little longer to get out of the car. By the time I got out of the car an argument started between Sammy and Lynn. Lynn locked the boys in his car and started to back out of the parking space. I started screaming at Lynn to let the boys out. The boys were crying and screaming from the back seat...

'Mommy, Mommy, get us out. We can't get out I kept screaming and begging and now banging on the car windows to let the boys out. The boys started crying louder. Lynn stopped the car. My oldest was able to unlock the back door and ran to my car. He got in my car and locked the door. Lynn was so angry and started cursing at me. "Pop!" I was still trying to get my baby out the car when I saw the trunk open. All I thought was he's got a gun. Is he crazy? He wouldn't do that in front of the boys? He pulled out a tire iron and came at me with full force. I froze. I couldn't believe what I was seeing. I couldn't move. It was like I was in some slow-moving motion picture. I put my arms up as to protect myself, as Lynn got closer to me and just before he put that crow bar to my throat, Sammy jumped in between us and then Lynn started swinging the tire iron around. Sammy called my name and told me to grab the baby and get to my car.

The managers of the McDonalds came out and told them to stop and that she was calling the police.

Sammy told him "Back off. 'Leave her alone man. You don't want your boys to remember you like this,' The police arrived and pulled Lynn back and he started yelling my name and saying, 'That's my wife. Those are my kids. That's my wife.'

I couldn't believe he was saying that. Since when did I become his wife again? He's been with every woman he could be with since we split up. I tried not to cry for the boy's sake. I needed to be strong. But I broke down in front of the cops and when the cops asked what happened I just tried to pull it together enough for them to understand what I was saying. Sammy stayed in the car while I spoke to the cops to keep the the boys company and keep them calm. I told the cops what happened and they suggested I get a restraining order. They wrote up a report and left. I will never forget the faces on my children when I finally got into the car. They were so afraid, confused and hurt. A hurt that would not go away for a very long time.

As I continued with my story, a Bible verse came to mind: Proverbs 14:14, *Backsliders get what they deserve; good people receive their reward.*

"God is my rock, my strength. My glorification. He has taught me to be strong and remain faithful in His name. God never abandoned me. I abandoned him. He waited patiently for me. He always protected me even when I didn't know I needed Him to. That is what true love is all about."

As my talk drew closer to an end, I started to feel closer to a healing, a closure of sorts. The many burdens and sorrows I had suffered were slowly lifting away.

"By knowing and feeling God's love, I was able to recover some of my dignity and respect. I knew that God had been with me throughout all these ordeals. All I had to do was call out to Him and let Him know I love Him and thank Him for never leaving my side.

As the tears rolled down my face, I read Isaiah 45:5, "I am the LORD: there is no other God. I have equipped you for battle, though you don't even know me.

"Lord God, I know You now. I know what You've done for me. I understand the sorrows I've had to suffer to be the woman and mother I am becoming or have become. I never want to lose my faith in You, Lord. I know You will never leave and during my darkest hours is when I know You are carrying me.

"Thank you, Jesus, for your unbinding love. Thank you, ladies, for listening to my story. May the grace of God fill your hearts with peace and love."

After I finished my talk and as I was led away to the chapel, the women clapped for me and two of my dearest friends came and hugged me with tears in their eyes. They congratulated me and told me how proud they were of me.

God took over that day and spoke through me to those women. That was where my path of growing faith to be closer to God began.

Chapter 14

"My child, when you are ill, do not delay, but pray to the Lord, and he will heal you."
—*Sirach 38:9 (NRSVCE)*

sat in my car and just stared out the window. Even as I was walking to my car I was in total disbelief. I couldn't have heard the doctor right. He's got to be wrong. I've gone through so many test, that my head started spinning like the girl in the movie "Exorcist." As the Doctor broke down every test result to me, I began to think what the hell does all this mean?

"We have to do surgery ASAP. We need to find out exactly what it is and if it's cancerous. I'll be scheduling the surgery for next week." The doctor said it would be an in out surgery and that he needed to do a biopsy and the results will take two weeks to get back. There will be some pain involved because they would literally be cutting out of me.

Two weeks? I thought to myself. Is he insane? How am I going to be able to wait two weeks to find out if I have cancer or not?

I began crying and screaming in the car. It's not fair. It's not right. None of this makes sense. When does it end?

I had been bleeding non-stop for almost a year. I wasn't able to go to a doctor because I had been laid off and had no insurance. I finally started working and after three months was eligible for health insurance. I finally went to the doctor for my annual physical and that's when I told him about my bleeding.

He sent me for half a dozen tests. Sonogram, histogram whatever kind of gram. I was tired of getting stuff stuck inside of me in a not so enjoyable way.

I didn't expect to hear what I heard. I was in total shock. What was I going to do, say to the family? My job? To the boys?

My parents had just left for a two week cruise and there was no way I was going to interrupt that cruise for them nor want to bring back the memory of when Abuela died and we had to call and get their cruise cut short.

When I got to my job, I told my boss what I was informed about. That they would be calling me today to inform me of when the surgery would be taking place. She seemed understanding and noted that I was quite worried about it. She talked to me for a bit and tried to calm my nerves.

A few hours later, I received the call from the doctor's office. The surgery was scheduled for the following Friday. The day my parents returned from their cruise. It was scheduled for 3:00 p.m. I had to get some blood work done before and would need to fast for twenty-four hours before. I was just moving like I was a puppet, someone else was in control.

The days before the surgery, I confided in my church sisters and ask that they put me in prayer. I called my son who was away at college. I worried about telling him as I knew he was going into final exams soon and needed to finalize papers, etc. We did some general talking and told him I had been to see a doctor and I had to have surgery. I told him about the cancer, etc. and I reassured him that everything was going to be alright and not to worry. He, so very calmly said to me, "Mom, I know it will. God is with you and I fear nothing. I'll keep you and the doctors in my prayers, but you'll be fine because you're the strongest woman I know." From the mouth of babes, although he's not a baby anymore. He was a young man. But will always be my baby and he was always good at encouraging me and knew when to say the right things.

⊷⟾⊸

He was about eight years old and was in his first year of pee-wee football. He was so adorable when he put on his football equipment. The pads were bigger than his head. He was so excited that first year of football. He was so driven, dedicated and excited about playing football like his big brother. I was feeling very low this particular day, a relationship I was in was just ending and I was very sadden and depressed about it. I had forgotten he had practice that day and he came in my office all dressed ready to go, until he saw my face. He asked if I was okay and I said that mommy wasn't feeling too good. That I was sorry, I forgot and could he skip practice today. He came to me hugged me and said it was Okay. A little bit after, his father called and they were talking about football and he asked why he wasn't going to practice. He told his father, "Mommy couldn't take me today." Well the next question his father asked got him a little upset because he immediately said, "Mommy, deserves a break sometime. She gets tired and deserves it." I looked up and tears welled up in my eyes. I couldn't believe he said that. He's always been very direct, but he told him. "I have to go now, Bye" and off he went. My son understood me. He knew and he felt it. After he hung up the phone I grabbed him and gave him a big hug and kiss and told him that I loved him and was so proud of him. He gave me a hug back, kissed me and said he loved me too. He was my little savior that day and my spirit just rose right after that.

So when he said this this time, he knew I was going to be Okay, he really believed it which gave me so much encouragement and kept me calm.

I then had to tell my oldest son. I wasn't too sure about how he would take the news. He wasn't quite as strong in his faith as my youngest one was so, I wasn't sure of what his reaction would be. I sat him down and explained the procedure to him and I tried to be upbeat and positive but his face said it all. You would have thought I just told him I was dying. I quickly grabbed him back to reality and re-explained saying it was just a test. I told him he had to take me to the surgery because it was an in-out surgical center and I really needed him with me. He said Okay, but I wasn't too convinced he was going to be able to deal very well with it.

Next was my brother. Since my parents weren't going to be back until the day of the surgery, I had to have a back-up plan just in case. So, I called my brother and began to explain the situation to him. He was another one; I knew he would take it hard. He and my oldest son favored each other a lot regarding issues like these. He got really quite over the phone and I had to call his name several times before he would answer me. He couldn't believe what he was hearing, but he understood. I told him my oldest would be with me to contact him, but that I would call him as soon as I could. He understood and told me he loved me. He was a bit upset with me however, because I waited until the night before the surgery to say anything to him, but I explained that I didn't want him to worry for longer than he had to. I was already doing that. While he understood it didn't lessen his worry.

My oldest son went out that night and he had not returned that morning. I kept calling him asking him when he'd be home. He said he'd be home in time to take me to the hospital. He wasn't dealing well at all with this. I knew it too. He stayed with a friend for the night as I knew he probably would. I knew he was upset.

After I couldn't sleep anymore, I got up and started cleaning my house just to try to keep my mind off upcoming events. I was playing one of my retreat CD's and one song hit me so hard; I got on my knees and started singing and praising God. The song ironically enough was, "On Bended Knee". I cried, I laughed, I prayed and I was finally at peace. Mami called within minutes. "Hey mama, we're off the ship and are on our way to the bus. How are you?"

Not wanting to tell her the minute she got out of her vacation, I engaged in small talk with her. Asking about the cruise, did she have a good time, anything exciting happen, etc.? I did everything I could to keep my voice steady and in control, because all mothers know when something is wrong with their children. Thank God I just sang, I thought to myself.

My son walked through the door two hours before I needed to go to the hospital. I didn't get it at first. One of my church sisters was to meet me at the hospital from work. She called to see how I was doing. I told her I was a nervous wreck. She informed me that she was about to leave work early and would meet me at the hospital. I told her what my son had done and I was a bit upset about it. She mentioned something I hadn't really considered — he was scared. He doesn't want to think about what could happen and he just needed to get away and not to be mad at him. As we hung up, I reminded her how much I appreciated her and thanked her for being there for me. "See you soon," she said.

As we walked into the surgical center, I started looking for someplace to sit and wait, but my son spotted it first and we sat down, with him next to me. He looked tired, worried and probably even scared a bit. We barely talked. He seemed to not know what to say. My girlfriend showed up and we hugged. She spoke to my son and we sat and just talked until my name was called.

"Hey mama, how you feeling?" I could barely open my eyes and keep them open.

"Where am I?" I asked.

"In recovery."

I felt a little bit of pain at first, but as I became more alert the more pain I felt. I asked for my son, but my girlfriend said she sent him home. He looked drained and felt it best for him to rest at home as I would probably need him later.

As we left the surgical center I thought about how I would have to wait what seemed like an eternity to get the results. We stopped for Chicken soup and to drop my prescription off and went home. My son would have to go get the prescriptions when they were ready. In the meantime, he came and got me from the car and tucked me in bed. But before knocking out for the night, I had to call Mami. She would be wondering why I hadn't call to see if they got home Okay. So I called to check up on her and she was too tired to talk so we hung up rather quickly feeling relieved that I didn't have to say anything tonight. Off to sleep I went.

The next morning I got up early and called Papi. I knew he'd be up early, as Mami loved to sleep in. I told Papi everything. The doctor's thoughts, the testing's, the surgery, but most of all the fact that I may be carrying around cancer cells and results wouldn't be back for another two weeks. We decided not to tell Mami. No need to get her all worried and maybe needlessly. So we would wait.

The next two weeks were hell and the doctor was true to his timeline. So I went to my doctor's appointment as scheduled. I had Endometrium (Uterine Polyps) and they were huge and in addition, my uterine wall had what looked like a cat crawled inside me and scratched my walls. Long lines in the uterine wall were totally abnormal. They were crevices within the wall with what appeared to be small cell within the lines. The doctor wasn't sure what it was and another surgery had to be done immediately. The difference this time was that not only would he remove the polyps but he would have to burn my uterine wall. Meaning, I would never be able to have children again. That's when all logic went out the window. I heard nothing after that. Okay, okay, but they are just tied. My tubes are just tied. Not cut or burned. I did that on purpose. Just in case I got married again and I wanted children with my new husband. I always wanted more kids, a little girl possibly. But this…..not having more children. I froze. I asked the doctor, "Why? Why did it have to be like this?"

"You are hosting cancer cells. If we don't do this procedure, it could turn into uterine cancer. Do you really want that? Did you really have plans for more children?"

That wasn't the point. I left again with another promise for a call with a surgery date. "But this time be prepared to take more time off than just a day" the doctor said. I was going to need at least two to three weeks off from work. FMLA was what I needed to do.

This time I called Mami and told her everything. From the first doctor's appointment to the first surgery to the results that doctor gave that day.

"Mami, but I will never be able to have kids again."

"Ay nina, please. Did you really want more kids? Your life is more important. Plus you already have two great kids."

That night, as I lay in bed, I cried myself to sleep. It is so unnatural to me to stop the process of birth. Only God should be able to do that. Now a doctor was going to cut all ways of me being able to birth a child. It wasn't fair I thought to myself. I would never feel another child grow inside of me again. Never rub my belly or give birth again. The thought sadden me so much that the tears kept rolling down my eyes until my eyes fell into a deep sleep in the land of dreams filled with sweet beautiful babies.

Chapter 15

"So David sent messengers to get her, and she came to him, and he lay with her."
—2 Samuel 11:4 (NRSVCE)

o he didn't. That's not what happened."

"Based on what you just told me, he raped you. It was date rape."

I was in denial and for the first time in fifteen years, it hit me like a ton of bricks. And of all people to help me realize it was my boyfriend.

⊷═◉

I met Angelo through a non-profit organization I had been working with in helping people start their own business. I had utilized this organization to start my own successful business and I wanted to give back to others.

He was smart, good background but most of all cute. I had seen him somewhere before and once we started talking we realized we had some friends in common.

We started working together in getting his business promoted and we formed a friendship, in fact did some dating here and there. He had just broken up with a girl he was considering marrying but we never got into the details and since he wasn't volunteering information, I never pried into it.

We hadn't seen each other in a while and ironically ran into each other at some event. We sort of picked up where we left off and even started a relationship of some sort. Nothing really serious, but enough to know that we couldn't share with others in our work group as it may have seemed favoritism was in play. We figured it would cause some conflicts and we preferred to avoid any problems. While nothing came of the relationship, we stayed in touch and checked on each other from time to time.

It was Valentine's Day and I was actually surprised to hear from him. I was never into Valentine's Day as that was the day I was married on and therefore avoided anything having to do with that day. Angelo called to wish me a Happy Valentine's day. He asked to take me to dinner and I agreed to go since I didn't have any plans anyway and I hadn't seen him in a while.

Well, dinner time came and went and as the time passed I just figured he got caught up in something and forgot about me. No biggie. We really weren't a couple and I didn't think much of it. As I was getting the boys ready for bed and call it a night with a movie, Angelo called saying he was sorry and that he was on his way. I explained to him it was late and I was getting the boys ready for bed, but there was something in his voice that was off and he was so insistent on seeing me, almost begging, so I agreed to let him come over.

As I was putting the boys to bed, Angelo arrived. "I already ate and I'm not hungry and its Valentine's Day and I don't have anyone to watch the boys." I said. "That's okay; I know there's a restaurant around the corner. Only for a little while, I promise." Well, I agreed to go and spoke to the neighbor's daughter to keep an eye out for the boys and she said she would. I told Angelo, "No more than an hour to an hour and a half." "Ok, Okay, I promise, no more." So off we went.

As we got into the car to go to the restaurant, I noticed him acting kind of funny and asked him what was up. He said he was fine and he grabbed me and proceeded to kiss me. I was surprised, because he threw me off guard. When we arrived at the restaurant we sat at the bar and Angelo in a matter of an hour had about three to four drinks. I was shocked and wondered what the hell was going on. I asked him to take me home.

"But why, I thought we were having a good time?" he said.

"It's been a little over an hour and I need to get home. Are you going to take me or do I have to walk?"

We got in the car and home we went.

I checked on the boys to be sure they were ok as Angelo waited downstairs for me. As I went downstairs an eerie feeling came over me and I knew I had to ask Angelo to leave. When I got downstairs, I noticed that he had put a rose on the counter and when I asked where it came from, he said, "I bought it for you." I really knew he was up to something then. I talked to him for a few minutes to see where his head was at but he kept saying weird stuff that didn't make any sense. We hadn't seen each other in a while and he was making comments about how good I looked but in a devouring way, not a sincere way. I couldn't explain it. Then he asked me to sit down, when I said I was fine standing, that's when it went in a totally different direction. He grabbed me down onto the couch and sat on top of me. He had me pinned down. I looked into his eyes and didn't like what I saw. I asked him to get off me and he began to kiss me roughly and fondle me aggressively. I asked him to stop. To please stop. He didn't listen. All of a sudden the phone rang. He stopped for a minute and that's when I had to think fast, I said it's probably my mother and she'll keep calling until I answer the phone, so please let me answer it. He allowed me to get up but he held onto my wrist so I wouldn't or couldn't say anything. But as I got to the phone the caller had hung up. I had no idea who it could be at that point and he had a look of satisfaction on his face. He proceeded to pull me down to him again, but the phone rang again.

"I'd better answer that quickly because she'll worry and I told you she'll keep calling until I answer. He allowed me to answer this time. I answered the phone and told Mami, I was tired and going to bed. I would call her tomorrow.

When I hung up the phone Angelo grabbed me again and had this look of confusion on his face. He said, "You want it. You know you do." I said, "No, No, Not like this." That's when he got mad and asked why all of a sudden, didn't I want him. He became very agitated and aggressive. I realized then that he wasn't just going to voluntarily leave, and he grabbed me down again and started to have sex with me roughly. Thinking quickly I suggested we go upstairs to my room where we would be more comfortable. He seemed happy about that and instantly got up to go to the stairs. But he hesitated for a minute as he finally released his grip on me, but pushed me ahead of him as we went up the stairs.. He followed me to my bedroom. I pretended to lock the door as he told me to do as he climbed between the sheets. He started kissing me but in his drunken stupor he started to fall asleep. Just as I was hoping he would. He started to snore but he woke himself up and started with me again. This time I laid him on his back and started kissing him, this time I was in control and I started caressing him. He fell back to sleep. My brain started racing. How was I going to get him out of here I thought to myself? I'm afraid the boys would wake up and I didn't want them to see this. I didn't want them to wake up to see me being hurt.

As I thought about the boys that was when it hit me. I would say that one of the boys is sick and they knocked at the door crying. So I slipped out of bed, opened the door and shut it hard enough for him to hear it. "What, What is going on?" "You're going to have to leave. One of my boys is sick. He is running a fever and I'm going to have to take care of him."

That's all it took. He got up and was moving about groggily but I helped him get dress, down the stairs and out to his car. He didn't say a word but he did look back at me and his look was like one of despair, embarrassment and shame. I never did figure that look out.

It was six hours of chaos. I couldn't believe what had happened. I had never been in a situation like this before and I was going to make damn sure it never happened again. I never saw him like that before and didn't know what to do. I immediately jumped into the shower and tried to wash him off me. I then proceeded to change the sheets and I ran downstairs to clean the area of carpet he forced me on. I didn't want any remains of him around me.

When I went back to bed I was exhausted but couldn't sleep. I just kept looking at my ceiling with disbelief. How did I let this happen? Why did I let this happen? I started trying to rationalize the situation. Did I lead him on? Did I do something to show I wanted it? I must have, otherwise why did he come at me this way? Did I deserve it?

Beep, Beep, Beep.....the alarm is going off. "Oh no, I'm going to be late. As I rushed to get ready and get the kids ready and shove them in the car, I noticed a card on my windshield. It was a Valentine's Day card from another guy that I had just started dating. He was a cop and had to work that night, which is why I didn't see him. That's when the tears finally came...

Chapter 16

❋

*"Above all, maintain constant love for one another, for
love covers a multitude of sins."*
—1 Peter 4:8 (NRSVCE)

Junior and I had known each other for most of
our lives, but just didn't know it.

We met again through a mutual friend on Facebook
and he inquired about me. He invited me to befriend him
and we started talking. Turned out that my parents knew
his parents and vice versa. We started talking almost every
day over the phone. The biggest problem we had is that he
lived about five hundred miles from me.

A number of weeks went by and an opportunity presented itself for us to meet face to face. It was Mother's Day weekend and my parents were interested in seeing him after so many years.

I drove up to my parents and Junior got a hotel close to my parents. So I went to meet him for the first time after all these years and bring him to my parent's house. As I walked down the hall to his room the butterflies in my stomach started flying around. He opened his room door and he started walking toward me. He was shorter than I thought which was a bit of a surprise and at first didn't know what to think. He led me to his room as I wanted to see how he kept his stuff. He was Neat and Organized.

As we got into his room he instantly started kissing me and it was nice at first, but a little fast I thought. We talked for a bit, but things got heated up fast, so I told him my parents were waiting for us so we better go.

My parents were excited and happy to see him after all these years and caught up pretty quickly with his family, etc. He was a handsome man for his age. He was about five years older than I was. I'm used to dating younger men. So this was a new thing for me.

We went with my parents to their community center for some dancing and to meet some of my parent's friends. Junior resembled this famous actor so my mother began introducing him as a look alike. All the women fell for it as he looked so much like this actor that they even shared the first same name. I loved the attention we got as we looked like a perfectly matched couple. As the day went on, we talked more about where we wanted to go with this relationship.

"So, what do you think" Junior said.

"About what?"

"This. Us. You and me?"

I knew what he was talking about; I just wanted to hear him say it. "I think we should give it a try," I said. "I like what we have and my parents seemed to like it to."

So we officially started dating that day.

⊷≡⊚

On my first visit to his house, I was a nervous wreck. It was a quick forty-five-minute flight, but none the less nerve wrecking.

I wanted to be sure I looked good, had the right clothes on, etc.

He met me at the end of the gate. He was so excited to see me. He had flowers and my heart melted. He was so genuine and real. He kissed me so long and hard, people were staring at us and saying "Get a room."

I was so excited to see him and my heart couldn't stop racing. As we drove to his house, he couldn't stop touching me, caressing me and looking at me. But he had this look of "I can't believe you're really mine." He was so amazing and totally into me. I so missed that from a man.

The weekend was amazing. We made love non-stop barely eating or drinking. He took me to the zoo, to his job to see where he worked and he kept taking pictures of me all weekend long. He said "this will be the only way I can see you every day."

We were going into our third month together and he asked me about love and being in love. I told him that I was falling in love with him and that it just felt right. I also told him to take his time as I didn't expect him to feel the same way right away even though I knew differently. He said he showed some pictures he had of me to some of his friends and they thought that "I had the look of love" in the pictures. I figured he must be looking for clarification from me.

"I've got to get back to work. I have a client waiting to see me. One more hour. I'll call you on my ride home." We hung up.

"Junior, what's wrong? We just hung up." He never calls right back, so I thought he was in an accident. He was just telling me how much traffic there was on the road a few minutes before we hung up.

"I'm in love with you too! And I couldn't wait to tell you."

"What? Junior, you don't have to say that to me just because I did."

"I know. But I mean it. I really do. I just didn't know how to say it to you."

We both just started laughing and as we got off the phone, we said at the same time, "I love you."

As I drove home that night, I felt exuberated. So excited that I couldn't wait to give him a call. We talked for hours and planned out our future together as it had been such a long time since either of us felt the way we did. I was in love.

Chapter 17

"Surely vexation kills the fool, and jealousy
slays the simple."
—Job 5:2 (NRSVCE)

*W*hat are you wearing?"
"I have on this dress I wore for my son's graduation it's a long pink and white sun dress."

"Take a picture of you; I want to see how you look. I miss you. Wish I could be there."

It was my birthday and was going to see Junior next week. I was doing a girls night out and we had to wear a flower in our hair. It was a Hawaiian theme restaurant so we all went in the closet thing to Hawaiian attire. I was excited to be hanging out with my favorite sisters. So, I went into the bathroom and took a picture for Junior to see how pretty I looked. One of my girlfriends was on her way to pick me up.

"I don't like that dress, you're showing too much."

"What are you talking about?"

"Your tits are hanging out all over the place. I can see them through the mirror."

"Ok, well, I can put a tank top underneath."

"No, you have to wear something else."

Our first fight and over something I was wearing. It was my birthday. How could he be so inconsiderate and act to ridiculous.

"If you wear that, we are over."

I argued with him telling him that I'm just going to be with a bunch of girls to dinner, that he was being ridiculous and he had to trust me. That there was nobody else I wanted, etc.

Even though we got through that fight, there were several more and a break up or two. But I thought after he went on the men's retreat a year later he would be different.

I prayed for him to be more patient and understanding to allow the love of God in his heart. That whatever pain and suffering he had gone through as a child be healed and to be a better man.

We had talked about getting engaged during Christmas and plan the wedding for the following summer. I had been looking for a job where he lived. He lived five hours from me, but he said he couldn't live without me and his job was with the government so he wouldn't be able to transfer to me so I had to go to him. For over six months I tried to find a job with no luck. But I had to get another job, so I found one where I lived with the idea that I would continue to look where he was and when I found one, leave the one I just got.

"Why would you do that?" Junior said.

"Because I was about to be laid off with all these cut backs. I needed something solid and better. That could be the reason I haven't found anything now." I said.

While he didn't like it he knew what I was talking about. Jobs were hard to come by due to the economy and I needed a better paying job.

We continued to travel back and forth to see each other every other weekend and enjoyed every opportunity we saw each other.

He would have his moments where he would get frustrated with the distance but I was always able to calm him down and tell him that there were families split apart for months and years and thank God we weren't separated like that. We could still talk over the phone and Skype each other every day.

On one visit to his house, I went to pick up dinner.

"Is that Juniors' car?"

"Excuse me?" I said.

"Is that Junior Rivera's car?

"Yes, it is."

"Oh, well tell him Linda said hi."

"Sure will. Good night."

As I drove away, I could see Linda in her car moving her chicken neck while on the phone, obviously talking shit about me.

"Hey baby. Did you get the food?"

"Yes, I'm driving back now. Who's Linda?"

"Who?"

"L.I.N.D.A"

"Oh, that's my ex-girlfriend. You know the one I told you about whose parents live across the street. Why?"

"She told me to tell you Hello."

"What, you saw her at Chili's?"

"Yes, she seemed a bit pissed off needless to say."

"Well, I never called her back nor did I leave her a message to say it was over."

"Are you serious?"

"Baby, she was crazy. Remember, I told she ran into the Ace Hardware store looking for me, screaming at the top of her lungs, etc."

"Junior, really. I'm almost home. We'll talk in a few."

When I got into the house, he had set the table with wine and music was playing. He was trying to smooth the issue away. He of course won.

I just wanted to hear what he had to say about the whole thing and I suggested he may want to keep his cars inside the garage for a while. She may want to slit his tires. We laughed about it, but I was serious.

I felt like we had grown closer that night, but apparently not as close as I had thought or wanted to.

138 ⪢ T.L. León

Junior drove for the first time to Miami. It was Father's Day weekend and I had a special weekend planned. He wasn't really good with directions and I had brought him a GPS to help make it easier for him. One of the reasons I don't like dating older guys. They swear they don't need help with anything.

He was almost at my house but got lost and my boss was in my office when he called. I didn't take the call, but as soon as my boss left. I called Junior back.

"I'm lost."

"Ok, where are you?" I was able to guide him home and told my son to let him in since he was home.

He jumped off the couch and ran to me when I walked through the door. It was like he hadn't seen me in years. It had only been two weeks. We had the time of our lives as I took him to different places in the area and we did the beach thing, because we both loved the beach. It was Sunday and time for him to leave. We said our goodbyes and planned for the next two weeks. I was going to fly up this time.

"Hey baby, I'm on my way home from work."

"Damn, it's three o'clock already. I've been so busy I haven't kept track of the time."

"How was work? Hope you weren't too tired on that drive home yesterday."

We talked for about fifteen minutes until he got home. We hung up and I told him I'd call him on my ride home.

Minutes later, I got a text from Junior. It was no ordinary text and it was super long. As I started reading the text, my heart started to beat fast, my head started spinning and I started to hyperventilate.

What the hell is this? Is he serious? I don't get it? He's breaking up with me via text. After almost two years of this back and forth, dealing with his insecurities, going to the men's retreat (which I paid for), the great Father's Day weekend we just spent together and he says' he can't take it anymore. He's done. What the fuck?

I tried calling him, he didn't answer. I tried texting him, he didn't answer. I tried everything to get his attention. After repeat calls to him he finally answered.

"There's nothing to talk about. I've made up my mind."

"What do you mean you made up your mind? What the hell does that mean? Junior, what's going on? Why are you doing this? We had such a great weekend. You went to the men's retreat not even a month ago and stood up there in front of everyone saying I was the love of your life and you would never leave me. I don't understand."

"It's over. That's it. That's all I got for you."

"Let's talk about this." Click. He was gone.

I cried just as much as when my husband left me. My heart broke into a million pieces. You had to pick me up off the floor with tweezers, that's how broken I was. I couldn't believe he would do this to me. To us. I couldn't think straight. My head was splitting in a dozen different ways. Okay, calm down. Stop crying. He'll call you back when he realized that he made a mistake. I'll wait. He must have had a bad day at work. Okay. Okay, that's it. Just be patient. He'll call.

He never called. I waited three days for him to call. Nothing. I tried to call him; it would go to voice mail. I finally called his sister. She said she didn't know and would call him and then call me back. She was just as flabbergasted as I was and didn't understand either. But she would get to the bottom of this. I knew she would.

A few hours later she called me. "Honey, I don't know what to tell you. He apparently can't take the distance and wants you with him now. twenty-four/seven."

"Mama, I can't just up and go. I have responsibilities here. In order for me to go I would need a job up there. He can't support two households and I don't know how long it would be before I found a job."

"I know, I know. He's always been this stubborn. I'll keep trying to talk to him. Give him a week or two. He may come around."

I kept trying to reach out to him. I even left him a message asking him to allow me to come up and get my things from his place and make love to him one more time. Well, that got his attention and he called me back.

"When are you coming?"

"Will we be able to talk?"

"I thought you wanted to say goodbye to me properly by making love for the last time and getting your shit?"

"Oh, is that all I am to you now? Then if we can't sit and talk about this whole thing, ship me all my stuff. I'm not just a piece of ass for you to stomp all over."

"Fine, I'll ship your stuff to you, but you don't want to be with me?"

"Junior, I do, but not just for some ass and it's over. How do you break up with someone over text? Really?"

"Well, your chose. Send me your address and I'll ship everything to you."

"No problem, I'll text it to you right now."

We hung up and I cried even harder. It's been three weeks since we last spoke and this is how he treats me.

The next morning I got up and found a shoe box and put the shit he left in my house, go figure, I must have at least three banker boxes at his house and all he has is a shoe box. What a shame, I thought to myself. He had only been to Miami three times since we started dating almost two years ago. Disgusting.

I went to work and looked for the closest post office to mail Junior his shit. At lunch, after a few seconds of hesitation, I sent the box along with all my love, hopes and dreams for $5.35.

Chapter 18

"...and forgive your people who have sinned against you,
and all their transgressions that they have committed
against you; and grant them compassion in the sight of
their captors, so that they may have compassion on them."
—1 Kings 8:50 (NRSVCE)

How many times had I read that verse in the bible? I have used it at least half a dozen times and I don't remember ever hearing the name of the man in the story. When she read that bible verse and his name was said, I knew right at that moment why I was here.

Lord, why do I still labor with this issue in my heart? Why does he still linger on my mind? Those were my first thoughts this morning? Really? Okay, I asked God last night before I went to bed that if he wanted me to go to the day of reflection tomorrow; he would wake me up on time to go.

I didn't want to go. I fussed about it, complained to anyone who would listen. My church sister, who was conveniently out of town this weekend, who knew I was struggling with it said, "Go, you may just get something out of it."

I thought, *Oh, please.* "I'm just about Jesus out," I said. And why would you do the day of reflection the weekend before the retreat. Now we had to get up two weekends in a row early. I obviously was not a morning person. I was certainly not feeling it. In addition, I found out the day started at 8:00 am. Why the hell did I think it started at 9:00 a.m.? No, no, no. I would get there when I get there. I saw the email late Friday night and I was exhausted. So I went to bed frustrated, but prayed to God saying, "I leave it to You."

7:25 a.m. Oh God, I'm just going to lay here five more minutes. I have to walk the dog, take a shower and make sure I get a load in the washing machine before I leave. Okay, check, check on this and check on that. Now I can go. It's now about 8:00 a.m. I guess I can go now. Things should have started good. I'm probably the last one there. I'm so stubborn and defiant sometimes. I don't always like following the rules. Can you tell, Lord?

The doors were locked. Oh, Hell no. If I had to walk to the side and start knocking on the doors... Oh, no. That wasn't going to work. Well, I guess I was not going in.

"Can I help you?" said one of the ushers, who must have been from another mass as I had never seen him before.

"Um, I'm part of the group. I'm trying to get in."

He unlocked the door and told me he had to lock the doors so that those not part of the group couldn't get in. I just listened and then walked in and sat in the last row in a pew by myself. Good, no one next to me except in the pew across the way and she already knew I had to leave. She was the co-leader of the upcoming retreat. I listened to the testimonies of the women giving the talks.

It became obvious they were talking about faith. It was a good testimony and I enjoyed hearing it.

Luke 8:40-48. I looked it up immediately. Oh my God, there is his name. That verse is my story. The bleeding woman. The two connected in this bible verse. I would have never thought about it before today. So I listened as she read the full scripture. okay God, I'm listening now. Boy, be careful what you wish for, because God is going to throw it at you, not when you want to but when He's ready to give it to you. So there were some questions we had to answer with the topic, but as I answered them, I kept going back to the scripture. Then it was time for the next speaker and the topic was on forgiveness. HOLY CRAP!!!!!

The speaker went on and on and on. She spoke about how good forgiveness felt and how it cleanses your soul. Then that's when she said it. "Is there anyone you need to forgive because they have hurt you in some way? Are you holding a grudge or resenting someone? That was it. That is really what it is. That is why I couldn't get him out of my head, out of my heart, out of my mind. I needed to forgive him. I needed to forgive him for picking his ex over me and letting me down over the holidays. He made me feel like he was going to make me pay for the pain his ex had put him through the holiday before. For making me pay for what his ex had done to him. I was angry at him because I was there for him when he needed someone to talk to about his issues days before that holiday he let me down. I was a true friend and he couldn't be that to me. I was there when he called. I was a real friend, but he didn't know what that was. I was truly hurt by that. I think that hurt me more than when we broke up. I was never able to tell him how it made me feel. But at that very moment, the clutter in my heart that I had over him had been emptied. My heart was cleared of the clutter. I forgave him right at that moment. I knew what I had to do. I texted him telling him I had to see him. He needed to know I forgave him. I had to tell him face to face. Not via text, not via voice mail or even email, but face to face because that's how a real woman does things.

⊸⫘⊙

"Hi everybody. Oh my God, it seems like forever. How is he doing?"

"He is in good spirits today. He has his family with him and now you're here, so he'll be excited to see you. You know, you'll always be his "Favorite Cadillac.""

I got that nickname years ago at a holiday party that lasted twenty-four hours. Somehow, my brother-in-law decided to name all his sister-in-laws after cars and mine was Cadillac.

"Where's Lynn?" I asked. "Is he here?"

"No, he went to the mall, but he should be here soon. He already called saying he was on his way back." One of my sister-in-laws said.

The boys were talking to their dying uncle, laughing and joking around with their other uncles and aunts. We received a tour of the new house since they just moved into that house a year before my brother-in-law was diagnosed with cancer. It was a shame as he wouldn't have much more time to enjoy the house. He was very thin from the medications and chemo he had received. While he aged tremendously from the disease, he was still his crazy, silly self.

After we toured the house, the boys went to play in the Video game room with their cousins.

"I have to tell you ladies something." As my sister-in-laws came in closer to hear what I had to say, I suspected that they would be surprised by what I was about to tell them. "I hadn't planned this, but it feels right and I want you to know what I'm going to do so you can help me get the family together." They listened intently. "I'm going to ask Lynn to forgive me for my part in the breakup of our marriage in front of the whole family."

"What the hell for? You didn't do anything. He should be apologizing to you for everything he has done to you." Gail said.

"Are you crazy? Why?" Carol said.

"Calm down, calm down. You'll see what I mean after it happens. Please just keep it to yourselves until it's time." They all agreed.

Within an hour my ex had arrived back to the house and I was very cordial to him and his wife. The boys spent some time with them and a million questions began between them. I just sat back, watched and listened.

After a while, a majority of the family was upstairs in the kitchen talking and that's when I knew it was time. I had already given two of the brothers a heads up and the wives had started to gather everyone together.

I asked my ex to have a seat and had the boys sit on either side of him. I then proceeded with my speech. I wasn't sure how to start, but I just started with the reasons and how we got to where we were. I took responsibility for the communication breakdown between us and how I wished things had been different.

"I forgive you for all the pain you caused me and I wish you nothing but the best always. And I'm sorry."

All eyes fell on him at that moment. All he said was "Okay. Is that it?"

"Yes, that's it." And he walked away.

Troy, his dying brother, called him low-class and how could he just sit there and say nothing. The boys even told him, "Dad, you aren't going to say something?" It didn't matter to me. I felt like a ton of bricks had just been lifted off my shoulders. I felt so free and relieved. It was an amazing feeling.

As the boys and I said goodbye, each family member came to me to express how proud and brave I was and how happy they were for me. I was elated by my new found freedom but sadden to say my final farewell to Troy as this would be his last holiday with us. He was slowly dying and he tried so hard to put a smile on his face for me. "You'll always be my baby sister-in-law and always "My Cadillac." As tears formed in my eyes, I kissed him good-bye for the last time ever.

·⊱═◉

He tried to call me back, but I couldn't answer. I was in the middle of listening to another talk and I didn't want to leave in the middle of it. It seemed rude and I tried to call him back on break, but he was at work, so I tried again a little while later, but no answer again. So I decided to text him. I received a text back saying he would call me later. Well, no call but I knew he had worked and he usually would get home tired so I didn't really expect a phone call after 9:00 p.m. So on Sunday after church I sent him another text — no response.

I ran into one of the organizers from the day of reflection the day before in front of the church. I shared with her what I was feeling and she told me to keep praying for him and that God heard me. If he didn't except or even want to hear it, that all that mattered was that God knew you had forgiven him. After she said that, I felt a sign of relief.

A few weeks later when I still hadn't heard from him, I sent him an email letting him know I forgave him and I wished him the best always, just like I did my ex-husband and the man who left me in pieces just the year before.

What I have learned over the years is that the way to a peaceful life, love and hope is to forgive those who have taken that away from me.

By allowing others to control those deep emotions for any amount of time, sucks you dry of these three basic components of life: PEACE, LOVE AND HOPE.

Peace of mind, with self and others.

Love of others, but most of all love for yourself, so others may love you.

Hope, in all your tomorrows that may or may not ever come.

But we must remember that after every storm there is a beautiful rainbow that always follows. And with that is a new beginning.

"The sadness they felt while they were apart, has turned into joy once more in each heart. They embrace with a love that will last forever, and then side-by-side, they cross over together." Retrieved from "The New Rainbow Bridge."

Acknowledgements

❋

First I want to say, T.G.B.T.G. — To God Be the Glory for without him none of this would have been possible.

To my parents who never gave up on me even when they thought they could, they always stood by me, providing me their opinions but also their everlasting love, encouragement and hope.

To my boys, you are the light of my life and I am so blessed to have been given you both as special gifts from God.

To my butterfly sisters, too many of you to name but you know who you are. Thank you for all your love, support, strength and never letting me bury myself under a rock and giving up.

To my niece, you are a mini-me. It's awesome to see you be a better image of me, and I love you so much for it. You are amazing.

To my brother and sister-in-law, you both have been a rock for me to stand on. You have supported me in more ways than one and I always feel your love from the hundreds of miles away.

To my nephew, go get them! Because your dreams will come true when it's the right time, never give up on them.

A special thanks to that undercover brother, RH for showing me the way and introducing me to this new publishing world, to PG for guiding me to him.

To all my other friends, family and extended family who helped build my life story. You all have played an intricate part in me being who I am today. I thank God for your support and love.

For those who have gone to join our heavenly father, you will always be in my heart.

T.G.B.T.G.